GLUTEN-FREE
BAKING

Published in 2020 by Bauer Media Books, Australia.
Bauer Media Books is a division of Bauer Media Pty Ltd.

BAUER MEDIA GROUP

Chief executive officer
Brendon Hill

Chief financial officer
Andrew Stedwell

BAUER MEDIA BOOKS

Publisher
Sally Eagle

Editorial & food director
Sophia Young

Creative director
Hannah Blackmore

Managing editor
Stephanie Kistner

Art director & designer
Jeannel Cunanan

Editor
Amanda Lees

Food editor
Sophia Young

Recipe developers
Elizabeth Fiducia, Rebecca Lyall, Nadia Fonoff, Tessa Immens, Sam Coutts, Kathy Knudsen

Operations manager
David Scotto

Business development manager
Simone Aquilina
saquilina@bauer-media.com.au
Ph +61 2 8268 6278

Printed in China
by 1010 Printing International

A catalogue record for this book is available from the National Library of Australia.
ISBN 978-1-92569-542-7

Published by Bauer Media Books, a division of Bauer Media Pty Ltd, 54 Park St, Sydney; GPO Box 4088, Sydney, NSW 2001, Australia
Ph +61 2 8116 9334;
Fax +61 2 9126 3702
www.awwcookbooks.com.au

International rights manager
Simone Aquilina
saquilina@bauer-media.com.au
Ph +61 2 8268 6278

Photographer
James Moffatt

Stylist
Steve Pearce

Photochef
Elizabeth Fiducia

Order books
phone 136 116 (within Australia)
or order online at
www.awwcookbooks.com.au

Send recipe enquiries to
recipeenquiries@bauer-media.com.au

THE AUSTRALIAN
Women's Weekly

GLUTEN-FREE BAKING

THE AUSTRALIAN WOMEN'S WEEKLY TEST KITCHEN
TRIPLE TESTED

CONTENTS

Food for EVERYONE

A gluten-free diet doesn't mean that you are relegated to a life without your favourite crusty breads, thin-based pizzas and other delectable baked goods. With some simple adjustments and armed with the recipes in this book it is possible to enjoy all these foods. Gluten avoidance goes beyond simply avoiding grains; care must also be taken to ensure gluten derivatives aren't present in seemingly innocuous foods, therefore it is imperative to read all labels very carefully. Gluten is a protein found in certain grains, principally wheat. However, it is also present in ancient wheat varieties too, including spelt and other grains such as rye and barley. Oats, though gluten-free, are problematic because of potential cross-contamination and they contain a protein similar to wheat which can cause reactions. While it is possible to purchase gluten-free oats, the current advice from Coeliac Australia is to avoid all oats and oat products unless under the supervision and testing of a medical practitioner – for this reason they have not been included in our book. It is the gluten in grains that absorbs water and gives structure to bread, pastries and other baked goods. Without it, it can be hard to achieve the exact same results in your baking.

In the absence of wheat and gluten-containing grains, what are the essential ingredients that you can bake with? There are a large variety of flours to call on, all with different textures, properties and tastes, easily sourced from large supermarkets. Ground nuts in all forms are useful, particularly for cakes and pastries, adding a rich buttery taste. Millet, buckwheat (not related to wheat), quinoa, lupin, besan (chickpea flour), sorghum, teff and amaranth are all nutritious options with defined earthy tastes. Less nutritious, but neutral-tasting flours are corn (maize), arrowroot, tapioca, potato and rice flour. All these flours can be used in various ways but they do not behave in the exact same way as ordinary flour, which is why flours are often mixed with one another to create the perfect balance in recipes.

Another useful ingredient for the gluten-free baker is xanthan gum. It is used as a thickener, emulsifier and stabiliser to compensate for what gluten would ordinarily do – provide structure and hold ingredients together. It can be quite a science making a gluten-free flour blend that mimics ordinary flour. For this reason a lot of the recipes in this book call for commercial gluten-free plain or self-raising flour, which are designed to be used 1:1 for regular flour.

We recognise that intolerances unfortunately work in tandem so have also marked recipes that are also dairy and nut-free. But above all, the recipes in this book are simply delicious whether you are coeliac, gluten sensitive or just simply love baking!

Perfect BAKING

We measure our cake pans across the top, from one inside edge to the other. Up your baking game by employing this and all our other useful tips and tricks when you are in the kitchen to gain the best results from our recipes. Read, measure, mix and bake! Enjoy!

Preparation & mixing

Don't wing things with baking - it's a science that relies on precision! Weigh or use metric measuring cups for ingredients. Don't pack ingredients into measuring cups (with the exception of brown sugar), simply scoop and level. Cream butter and sugar mixes with an electric mixer on medium speed, scraping down the side of the bowl. Egg whites should be room temperature and free of any egg yolk, and beaten in a clean bowl on high speed for maximum aeration. If no sugar is added, take care not to over beat them. If sugar is added, check that it is dissolved; the mix will look glossy and hold stiff peaks, and will feel smooth when rubbed between your fingers.

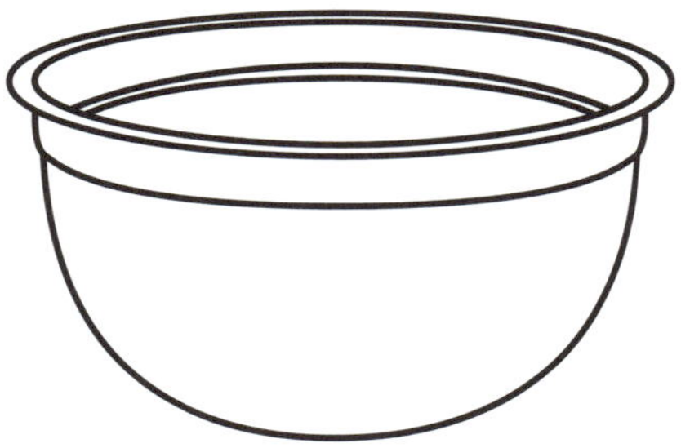

STORAGE

Gluten-free items stale faster, so freezing, if specified in the recipe, is a good option. Items must be cooled completely before storing in an airtight container or they will soften in the container. Filled biscuits and cakes are best filled on the day of serving. Cakes and tarts with dairy-based fillings must be refrigerated.

Q+A

CAN I SWAP SWEETENERS?

You will need to experiment, as the result will depend on the other ingredients in the recipe. Different types of crystalline sugar are fairly safe to swap, for one another. However, liquid sweeteners and low calorie types will change outcomes.

Oven trays

For even baking and browning of: biscuits, scones, sausage rolls and other baked items use flat aluminium trays, which have little or no sides. This enables the heat to circulate properly and ensures even browning. Grease trays lightly with cooking-oil spray or butter. To bake two or more trays at once, ensure trays don't touch the sides, or the door when it is closed. Keep at least 2cm (¾in) of space around each tray to allow good heat circulation. To cook evenly, swap trays around halfway through baking.

Q+A

I DON'T HAVE THE CAKE PAN THE RECIPE CALLS FOR WHAT SHOULD I DO?

If a recipe calls for a square cake pan and all you have are round, choose one that is 2cm (¾in) larger than the specified square. Conversely, if a round pan is required, substitute with a square pan 2cm (¾in) smaller than specified. Don't swap tube pans or the recipe may fail. Most large cakes can be baked as small in texas muffin pans.

Testing if cooked

Use a fine metal or bamboo skewer to test cakes and loaves for doneness. Insert the skewer into the centre, avoiding any cracks. Then look and touch the skewer to see if the mixture is dry. If the cake is to be fudgy, some recipes will specify 'with moist crumbs attached'. Another sign of doneness is that the cake will have pulled away from the side of the tin. For aerated cakes like a sponge, gently press the top; it should spring back when touched.

Q+A

HOW DO I ACTIVATE YEAST CORRECTLY?

The liquid added to your yeast should be warm (about 26°C) in order to activate it. If it is too cool, it will retard the yeast growth; too hot, it will kill the yeast. Combine dried yeast, sugar and the warm water in a jug until the yeast dissolves. Stand 10 minutes until frothy.

WHICH GLUTEN-FREE FLOUR?

Gluten free flours can be broken up into the following four categories – select the best one for your recipe needs. Protein is required for structure in loaves and pastry. In cakes, other ingredients such as eggs and xanthan gum can also assist in the absence of gluten.

- Gluten-free starches – pure corn starch (cornflour), tapioca starch, arrowroot starch and potato starch. These interchangeable starches can be used as thickeners in fillings for pies. To use, make a slurry with a little cold water before adding to a hot mixture; bring to the boil, stirring to thicken.
- Neutral tasting, low protein flours – rice, millet and cornmeal – are useful as carrier flours, but they lack structure for baking, so must be used in combination with other flours or thickening and binding agents.
- Earthy, low protein flours – teff, buckwheat, quinoa, and amaranth – provide a defined taste but no structure. For sweet baking temper with a neutral flour.
- High protein flours – besan (chickpea four) and soy flour – used alone can be very dense. These are best balanced with flours from the other groups. Besan flour however can be used to make delicious pancakes and a gluten-free batter.

OTHER TIPS

- Don't overbeat the butter and sugar mixture: stop when they are well combined but still firm. Overbeating makes the mixture too soft, causing biscuits to spread.
- To test if bread is done, firmly tap on the base; it will sound hollow when cooked.
- If you bake two or more trays of cakes at once, swap the trays around mid-way through baking, rotating them as well, to help with even browning.
- Biscuits should develop a crust, but still feel slightly soft to the touch when you remove them from the oven. They will firm up as they cool.
- Don't stack baked items on top of each other when cooling; they need air circulating around them to maintain their texture.

BREADS & PIZZA

Good with... HUMMUS AND DUKKAH, OR SMASHED AVOCADO, CHILLI FLAKES AND A SQUEEZE OF LEMON, OR SMEARED WITH BABA GANOUSH AND TOPPED WITH A HANDFUL OF CRISP BABY SALAD GREENS FOR CRUNCH.

Chickpea, caraway & CARROT BREAD

1 Preheat oven to 180°C/350°F. Line an oven tray with baking paper. Grease a 10cm (4in) deep, 11cm x 22cm (4½in xi 9in) loaf pan; line base and sides with baking paper.
2 Trim baby carrots leaving a little of the stalk attached, then halve each lengthways Place onto lined tray. Drizzle with oil; season. Roast carrots for 30 minutes or until softened slightly. Cool.
3 Meanwhile, grate large carrot coarsely; you will need 1 cup grated carrot. Place grated carrot into the bowl of an electric mixer. Add ½ cup of the chickpeas, the buckwheat flour, chickpea flour, psyllium husks, yeast, 2 teaspoons of the caraway seeds and the salt to the bowl. Combine 1¼ cups (310ml) water and the extra oil in a jug; add to dry ingredients. Mix using the paddle attachment on low speed for 1 minute or until a wet dough forms. Using buckwheat floured hands, transfer dough to a gluten-free flour-dusted work surface. Using your hands, shape dough into a 22cm (9in) log. Place into the loaf pan. Cover with a clean tea towel and leave for 1 hour or until risen by a quarter.
4 When loaf is ready to bake, place roasted carrots lengthways on top, and scatter with remaining chickpeas and caraway seeds.
5 Bake bread for 50 minutes or until golden brown and it sounds hollow when tapped. Cool bread in pan.

KEEPING Bread will keep in an airtight container in the fridge for up to 1 week or frozen for up to 1 month.

PREP + COOK TIME 1 HOUR 15 MINUTES (+ STANDING)
MAKES 1 LOAF (12 SLICES)

1 bunch heirloom baby carrots (400g)
2 teaspoons extra virgin olive oil
1 large carrot (180g), peeled
400g (12½oz) can chickpeas (garbanzo beans), drained, rinsed
1½ cups (225g) buckwheat flour, plus 2 tablespoons extra to dust
1½ cups (225g) chickpea flour (besan)
2 tablespoons psyllium husks
2 teaspoons (7g) dried yeast
3 teaspoons caraway seeds
2 teaspoons sea salt flakes
½ cup (125ml) extra virgin olive oil, extra

DAIRY FREE

Tea-soaked raisin & walnut
BREKKIE LOAF

4 english breakfast tea bags
1½ cups (225g) raisins
1 teaspoon raw caster (superfine) sugar
2 teaspoons (7g) dried yeast
2 tablespoons psyllium husks
1 cup (150g) buckwheat flour
¾ cup (85g) quinoa flour
¾ cup (90g) tapioca flour
2 teaspoons gluten-free baking powder
1 tablespoon mixed spice
¾ teaspoon fine sea salt
⅓ cup (75g) coconut oil, melted
1 cup (100g) walnuts, chopped coarsely

1 Place tea bags in a medium heatproof jug; pour over 2½ cups (625ml) boiling water, stand for 5 minutes. Add raisins to tea; soak for 15 minutes or until tea is lukewarm.

2 Combine ½ cup of the lukewarm tea liquid, sugar and yeast in a small jug; stir until yeast dissolves. Stand in a warm place for 5 minutes or until mixture is frothy.

3 Strain remaining tea into a large bowl; reserve raisins. Whisk psyllium husks into the strained tea liquid. Sift flours, baking powder, spice and salt over psyllium husk mixture; add yeast mixture and coconut oil. Stir to form a wet dough. Stir in 1 cup of the soaked raisins and ½ cup of the walnuts.

4 Lightly oil a 20cm (8in) domed-shaped mixing bowl (see tip). Scoop soft dough into bowl; cover with plastic wrap. Stand dough in a warm place for 1½ hours or until dough has doubled in size.

5 Preheat oven to 180°C/350°F. Line an oven tray with baking paper.

6 Tip dough out onto oven tray; scatter with remaining raisins and walnuts. Bake for 65 minutes or until loaf is golden and it sounds hollow when tapped, covering with foil halfway through cooking if overbrowning. (Bread will spread and flatten during cooking.) Cool.

TIP Proving this wet style dough in a dome-shaped bowl will allow the psyllium husks and flour to absorb some of the liquid and set the shape.

KEEPING Bread will keep in an airtight container at room temperature for up to 3 days or frozen for up to 1 month.

DAIRY FREE

EGG FREE

PREP + COOK TIME 1 HOUR 40 MINUTES (+ STANDING)
MAKES 1 LOAF (10 SLICES)

Good for... BREAKFAST WITH YOUR FAVOURITE SPREAD. SERVE FOR LUNCH WITH SHREDDED CHICKEN, A LITTLE STORE-BOUGHT AÏOLI AND A HANDFUL OF ROCKET OR FOR DINNER AS A TOASTIE WITH ANY LEFTOVERS AND MELTED CHEESE.

Basic gluten-free BREAD

1 Grease a 12cm x 20cm (4¾in x 8in) loaf pan; lightly dust with rice flour.

2 Combine sifted flours, yeast and gum in a large bowl. Crumble in half the salt.

3 Place whole egg, egg whites, oil, vinegar and 1½ cups (375ml) water in a large bowl of an electric mixer; beat on medium speed for 3½ minutes. Add ½ cup (125ml) water and the flour mixture, 1 cup at a time, beating until mixture is combined and smooth.

4 Spoon dough mixture into loaf pan; smooth the surface. Cover; stand in a warm place for 45 minutes.

5 Preheat oven to 220°C/425°F.

6 Drizzle loaf with extra oil then sprinkle with remaining salt. Bake for 1 hour or until crust is firm and golden brown and the loaf sounds hollow when tapped. Stand bread in pan for 5 minutes before turning, top-side up, onto a wire rack to cool.

TIP This mixture will make 6 gluten-free bread rolls – divide dough into 6 even portions, roll into balls and place on a greased and floured oven tray, then stand for 45 minutes. Drizzle rolls with oil and sprinkle with salt; bake for 30 minutes.

KEEPING Bread is best eaten the day it is baked, however, it's great for toast or toasted sandwiches the next day.

PREP + COOK TIME 1 HOUR 30 MINUTES (+ STANDING)
MAKES 1 LOAF (12 SLICES)

3 cups (405g) gluten-free plain (all-purpose) flour
½ cup (75g) potato flour
1 cup (160g) brown rice flour, plus extra for dusting
3 teaspoons (10g) dried yeast
2 teaspoons xanthan gum
2 teaspoons flaked sea salt or black salt
1 egg
3 egg whites
¾ cup (180ml) extra virgin olive oil
1 teaspoon white vinegar
1 tablespoon extra virgin olive oil, extra

DAIRY FREE

Basic BREAD VARIATIONS

4-SEED COB

PREP + COOK TIME 1 HOUR 30 MINUTES (+ STANDING) **MAKES** 1 LOAF (12 SLICES)

Make basic gluten-free bread on page 16, to the end of step 3. Add ¼ cup pepitas (pumpkin seed kernels), 2 tbsp sunflower seed kernels, 2 tbsp linseeds (flaxseeds) and 1 tbsp white chia seeds to dough; fold through dough. Using wet hands, shape dough into a 25cm (10in) round loaf on an oiled and baking-paper-lined oven tray. Drizzle with 1 tbsp olive oil and scatter with 1 tsp salt flakes. Cover loaf; stand in a warm place for 45 minutes. Preheat oven to 220°C/425°F. Bake for 50 minutes or until golden and loaf sounds hollow when tapped. Stand loaf on tray for 5 minutes before transferring to a wire rack. Serve warm.

THREE CHEESE BREAD

PREP + COOK TIME 1 HOUR 30 MINUTES (+ STANDING) **MAKES** 2 STICKS (24 SLICES)

Make basic gluten-free bread on page 16, to the end of step 3. Add ¼ cup coarsely grated vintage cheddar, ⅓ cup finely grated parmesan and 100g (3oz) crumbled fetta; fold through dough. Using damp hands, shape dough into 2 x 35cm (14in) long loaves on two oiled and baking-paper-lined trays. Cover both loaves; stand in a warm place for 45 minutes. Preheat oven to 220°C/425°F. Drizzle loaves with 1 tbsp olive oil and scatter with 1 tsp salt flakes. Cut three slits in the top of each loaf. Bake for 55 minutes or until golden and loaves sound hollow when tapped. Stand loaves on tray for 5 minutes before transferring to a wire rack. Serve warm.

GREEN OLIVE & THYME ROLLS

PREP + COOK TIME 1 HOUR 20 MINUTES (+ STANDING) **MAKES** 8 ROLLS

Make basic gluten-free bread on page 16 to the end of step 3. Add 1 cup thinly sliced pitted sicilian green olives and 2 tbsp thyme leaves; fold through dough. Divide dough into 8 portions. With wet hands, roll portions into balls. Place on an oiled and baking-paper-lined oven tray. Cover rolls; stand in a warm place for 45 minutes. Preheat oven to 220°C/425°F. Drizzle with 1 tbsp oil and scatter with 1 tsp salt flakes. Bake for 40 minutes or until golden and rolls sound hollow when tapped. Stand rolls on tray for 5 minutes before transferring to a wire rack. Serve warm.

TOMATO & BASIL LOAF

PREP + COOK TIME 1 HOUR 20 MINUTES (+ STANDING) **MAKES** 8 ROLLS

Make basic gluten-free bread on page 16, adding ¼ cup tomato paste to the wet mixture at the start of step 3. After the flour is added at the end of step 3, add ⅔ cup thinly sliced drained semi-dried tomatoes and ⅓ cup shredded basil leaves; fold through dough. Divide dough into 8 portions. With wet hands, roll portions into balls. Place on an oiled and baking-paper-lined oven tray. Cover rolls; stand in a warm place for 45 minutes. Preheat oven to 220°C/425°F. Drizzle with 1 tbsp olive oil. Bake for 40 minutes or until golden and rolls sound hollow when tapped. Stand rolls on tray for 5 minutes before transferring to a wire rack. Serve warm.

Teff IS A SEED WORTH GETTING TO KNOW IF YOU DON'T TOLERATE GLUTEN AS IT IS SUBSTANTIALLY MORE NUTRITIOUS THAN MANY GLUTEN-FREE FLOUR ALTERNATIVES. THIS TINY HIGH-PROTEIN SEED, OF A VARIETY OF COLOURS, IS MILLED TO PRODUCE IVORY OR BROWN TEFF FLOUR.

EGG FREE

Teff & olive LOAVES

3½ cups (470g) gluten-free self-raising flour
1 cup (160g) ivory teff flour
1 cup (150g) potato flour
¼ cup (40g) fine polenta, plus 1 tablespoon extra
2 tablespoons thyme leaves, plus 1 teaspoon extra
1 teaspoon xanthan gum
1 teaspoon bicarbonate of soda (baking soda)
2 teaspoons sea salt flakes
600ml buttermilk
⅓ cup (80ml) extra virgin olive oil
¼ cup (90g) honey
1⅓ cups (200g) pimento-stuffed green olives

1 Preheat oven to 180°C/350°F. Grease two 8cm x 18cm (3¼in x 7¼in) loaf pans.

2 Place flours, polenta, thyme, xanthan gum, bicarbonate of soda and salt in a large bowl of an electric mixer fitted with the paddle attachment. Whisk buttermilk, olive oil and honey in a large jug. Add liquid ingredients to dry ingredients. Beat on low speed for 1 minute or until mixture is just smooth. Fold through olives.

3 Transfer dough to a gluten-free floured surface; divide into two portions. Using damp hands, shape each portion into a 6cm x 12cm (2½in x 4¾in) oval loaf. Place loaves into tins. (Alternatively place 5cm (2in) apart on a large baking-paper-lined oven tray.) Dust with extra polenta and thyme leaves.

4 Bake loaves for 45 minutes or until crisp, browned and they sound hollow when tapped on base.

5 Transfer loaves to a wire rack, cover with a clean tea towel and leave to cool slightly. Serve warm with butter or avocado.

KEEPING Loaves will keep in an airtight container for up to 3 days. Serve toasted with butter in following days or freeze for up to 1 month.

PREP + COOK TIME 1 HOUR **MAKES** 2 LOAVES (24 SLICES)

Good for... PORTABLE SNACKS, LUNCH BOXES AND PICNICS. SERVE WITH A COUPLE OF CHEESES AND DIPS AS PART OF A GRAZING BOARD OR WITH SOUPY OR STEWY DISHES, TO MOP UP THE COOKING JUICES.

Kale & haloumi TWISTS

1 Grease two oven trays; line with baking paper.

2 Wash kale then tear leaves from stalks into small pieces; discard stems. Place leaves in a heatproof bowl. Pour boiling water over kale to cover; stand for 1 minute. Drain. Rinse under cold water; drain. Squeeze excess water from kale.

3 Combine sifted flours, yeast, salt and xanthan gum in a large bowl.

4 Place whole egg, egg whites, oil, vinegar and 1½ cups (375ml) warm water in a large bowl of an electric mixer; beat on medium speed for 3½ minutes. Add flour mixture, 1 cup at a time, beating until mixture is combined and smooth. Fold kale and haloumi through dough (the dough will be very wet).

5 Divide dough into eight portions. Using gluten-free floured hands, roll portions into 35cm (14in) rope shapes. Tie each shape into a knot then bring ends around the knot as pictured. Place twists on oven tray. Cover; stand in a warm place for 45 minutes.

6 Preheat oven to 220°C/425°F.

7 Sprinkle twists with fennel seeds. Bake for 40 minutes or until golden and sound hollow when tapped. Leave on tray for 5 minutes before transferring to a wire rack to cool. Serve warm.

KEEPING Twists are best eaten on the day they are made or freeze for up to 3 months.

PREP + COOK TIME 1 HOUR (+ STANDING) **MAKES** 8

1 bunch kale (250g)
3½ cups (470g) gluten-free plain (all-purpose) flour
½ cup (75g) potato flour
1 cup (180g) white rice flour
3 teaspoons (10g) dried yeast
2 teaspoons table salt
2 teaspoons xanthan gum
1 egg
3 egg whites
¾ cup (180ml) olive oil
1 teaspoon white vinegar
200g (6½oz) haloumi, grated
1 tablespoon fennel seeds

NUT FREE

EGG FREE

NUT FREE

Quinoa & buckwheat MARGHERITA PIZZA

1 teaspoon extra virgin olive oil
2 tablespoons white chia seeds
⅔ cup (140g) white quinoa, rinsed
1½ tablespoons buckwheat flour
1 teaspoon gluten-free baking powder
1½ tablespoons finely grated parmesan
a pinch of table salt
½ cup (140g) tomato passata
2 tablespoons finely shredded basil
¼ cup (20g) finely grated parmesan, extra
300g (9½oz) fresh mozzarella (fior di latte), torn
¼ cup basil leaves, extra

1 Preheat oven to 220°C/425°F. Line a 30cm (12in) round pizza tray with baking paper; brush paper with oil.

2 Combine chia seeds and ⅓ cup (80ml) water in a small bowl. Stand for 10 minutes or until thick.

3 Place quinoa, flour, baking powder, parmesan, salt, ⅓ cup (80ml) water and chia mixture in a high-powered blender. Blend until almost smooth, stopping the blender and scraping down the sides several times during blending. Spread mixture evenly over tray.

4 Bake pizza base for 15 minutes or until golden brown.

5 Spread combined passata and shredded basil on pizza base, leaving a 1cm (½in) border. Top with extra parmesan and half the mozzarella.

6 Bake pizza for 10 minutes or until cheese is golden and bubbling. Scatter with extra basil leaves and remaining mozzarella; season with pepper.

TIPS Pizza is best made close to serving. Double the recipe to make 2 pizzas, if you like.

PREP + COOK TIME 45 MINUTES (+ STANDING) **SERVES** 2

Pizza TOPPING VARIATIONS

ROCKET, PROSCIUTTO & PARMESAN PIZZA

PREP + COOK TIME 45 MINUTES (+ STANDING) **SERVES** 2

Make pizza base using recipe on page 25 to the end of step 5. Bake for 10 minutes or until cheese is golden and bubbling. Top with 100g (3oz) thinly sliced gluten-free prosciutto, 30g (1oz) baby rocket (arugula) leaves and 2 tbsp shaved parmesan.

HAM, PINEAPPLE & CHILLI PIZZA

PREP + COOK TIME 45 MINUTES (+ STANDING) **SERVES** 2

Make pizza base using recipe on page 25 to the end of step 5. Top pizza with 100g (3oz) thinly sliced gluten-free leg ham, 100g (3oz) thinly sliced fresh pineapple and ½ tsp dried chilli flakes. Bake for 10 minutes or until the cheese is golden and bubbling. Serve sprinkled with extra chilli, if you like.

CHARGRILLED VEG & GOAT'S CHEESE PIZZA

PREP + COOK TIME 1 HOUR (+ STANDING) **SERVES** 2

Make pizza base using recipe on page 25 to the end of step 5. Cook 100g (3oz) lightly oiled sliced orange sweet potato and 400g (12½oz) sliced eggplant in a heated oiled chargrill pan (or barbecue) for 3 minutes each side or until tender. Top pizza with 100g (3oz) thinly sliced drained chargrilled red capsicum (bell pepper), chargrilled vegetables and 50g (1½oz) crumbled marinated goat's cheese. Bake for 10 minutes or until the cheese is golden and bubbling. Serve pizza drizzled with 2 tbsp store-bought pesto.

BLUE CHEESE & ONION PIZZA

PREP + COOK TIME 1 HOUR (+ STANDING) **SERVES** 2

Heat 2 tsp olive oil in a large frying pan over low heat; cook 1 thinly sliced red onion and 1 tsp brown sugar, stirring occasionally, for 10 minutes or until golden brown. Make pizza base using recipe on page 25 to the end of step 5. Top pizza with 50g (1½oz) crumbled creamy blue cheese, 50g (1½oz) thinly sliced spicy gluten-free salami, 50g (1½oz) pitted kalamata olives and the caramelised onion. Bake for 10 minutes or until cheese is golden and bubbling.

PIADINA
with charred broccolini & mushrooms

1 Preheat oven to 180°C/350°F.

2 Process ricotta, goat's cheese, garlic, lemon rind, lemon juice and 2 tablespoons water until a smooth, spreadable consistency. Season; refrigerate until required.

3 Preheat a chargrill plate (or barbecue) over high heat. Trim ends from broccolini then cut thick stalks in half lengthways. Toss with 1 tablespoon of the olive oil; season. Chargrill for 2 minutes each side or until tips are lightly charred and broccolini is tender. Toss mushrooms with remaining olive oil; season. Chargrill for 1½ minutes each side or until tender.

4 Meanwhile, make flatbreads.

5 To serve, spread four flatbreads with goat's cheese spread (see keeping). Top with chargrilled broccolini and oyster mushrooms; season.

flatbreads Combine flours in a medium bowl; make a well in the centre. Add egg, half the oil and ¾ cup (180ml) water, approximately, to form a soft dough. Knead on a gluten-free floured surface until smooth. Divide dough into 10 portions; roll each portion into a 3mm (⅛in) thick, 20cm (8in) oval. Brush flatbreads with remaining oil; cook on a heated chargrill plate (or barbecue) for 3 minutes each side or until browned and crisp.

TIP Flatbreads are also great to use as pizza bases.

KEEPING Wrap remaining six flatbreads in plastic wrap and freeze for up to 3 months.

PREP + COOK TIME 1 HOUR 30 MINUTES
SERVES 4 (MAKES 10 FLATBREADS)

200g (6½oz) soft ricotta
200g (6½oz) fresh goat's cheese, crumbled
1 clove garlic, crushed
1 teaspoon finely grated lemon rind
2 tablespoons lemon juice
2 x 175g (5½oz) bunches broccolini
¼ cup (60ml) extra virgin olive oil
300g (9½oz) oyster mushrooms

FLATBREADS

1½ cups (225g) buckwheat flour
1½ cups (225g) 100% corn (maize) cornflour (cornstarch)
2 eggs, beaten lightly
2 tablespoons extra virgin olive oil

NUT FREE

Potato & rosemary FOCACCIA

1 Preheat oven to 200°C/400°F. Grease a large oven tray; line with baking paper, extending the paper 2cm (¾in) over the long sides.

2 Peel 300g (9½oz) of the potatoes, halve and place in a saucepan. Cover with cold water and salt. Bring to the boil. Cook potatoes for 18 minutes or until tender. Drain; stand in a sieve set over a saucepan for 15 minutes to dry out and cool completely. Push potato through a ricer or fine sieve into a medium bowl. Fold through whole egg, egg white, honey, and 2 tablespoons of olive oil.

3 Process cashews until finely chopped. Add flours, baking powder, salt and pepper; pulse until mixture is fine and combined. Transfer to a work surface and make a well in the centre. Add potato mixture to centre of the well. Using a butter knife, cut the wet ingredients through the dry ingredients until loosely combined. Using your hands, knead for 1 minute or until a smooth dense dough forms.

4 Transfer dough to lined tray. Using oiled hands, press and spread evenly on tray to form a 20cm (8in) wide, 30cm (12in) long oval shape. Thinly slice remaining 300g (9½oz) potato, using a mandoline, V-slicer or a very sharp knife. Toss potato in a bowl with remaining 2 tablespoons of oil and the rosemary leaves. Arrange over dough, pressing with fingers to push into dough slightly. Season with salt and pepper.

5 Bake focaccia in the top third of the oven for 30 minutes or until golden and sounds hollow when tapped on the base.

6 Cool on tray for 10 minutes then transfer to a board; drizzle with extra oil and sprinkle with parmesan to serve.

600g (1¼lb) sebago potatoes
1 egg
1 egg white
2 tablespoons honey
⅓ cup (80ml) extra virgin olive oil, plus extra to drizzle
2 cups (300g) raw cashews
1¼ cups (180g) tapioca flour
⅓ cup (50g) potato flour
1½ teaspoons gluten-free baking powder
1 teaspoon sea salt flakes
¼ teaspoon freshly ground black pepper
3 large rosemary sprigs, leaves picked
⅓ cup (25g) finely grated parmesan

KEEPING Focaccia is best eaten on the day it is made or freeze for up to 1 month.

PREP + COOK TIME 1 HOUR **SERVES** 6

Good for... BREAKFAST WITH CREAM CHEESE OR JAM, OR LUNCH WITH SMASHED AVOCADO, ROASTED CHERRY TOMATOES, CRUMBLED FETTA AND FRESH OREGANO LEAVES, OR... WITH WHATEVER YOU WANT!

Seeded BAGELS

3⅓ cups (450g) gluten-free plain (all-purpose) flour
½ cup (75g) potato flour
½ cup (90g) white rice flour
½ cup (75g) buckwheat flour
3 teaspoons (10g) dried yeast
2 teaspoons table salt
2 teaspoons xanthan gum
4 eggs
¾ cup (180ml) olive oil
1½ cups (375ml) warm milk, plus 1 tablespoon extra
2 teaspoons seeds or herb mix (see tip)

1 Combine sifted flours, yeast, table salt and xanthan gum in a large bowl.
2 Separate 3 of the eggs; reserve yolks. Beat remaining whole egg, the egg whites, oil and milk in a large bowl with an electric mixer on medium speed for 3½ minutes. Add the flour mixture, 1 cup at a time, beating until combined and smooth.
3 Turn dough onto a lightly gluten-free floured surface and knead until smooth. Divide dough into 10 pieces. Roll each piece into a ball. Push a finger through the centre of each ball and stretch it out slightly to form a 9cm (3¾in) ring. Place ring on an oiled oven tray. Repeat with remaining dough. Cover with oiled plastic wrap; stand in a warm place for 45 minutes.
4 Preheat oven to 200°C/400°F. Oil two oven trays then line with baking paper.
5 Working in batches of four, drop bagels one by one into a large saucepan of boiling water, ensuring they don't touch; boil for 1 minute. (The longer you boil the bagels the chewer they become.) Turn bagels over; boil for another minute. Using a slotted spoon, transfer bagels to lined trays. Repeat with remaining bagels.
6 Brush tops of bagels with combined reserved egg yolks and extra milk; sprinkle with seeds. Bake for 30 minutes or until golden. Cool on a wire rack.

NUT FREE

TIP You can use caraway seeds, sesame seeds, chilli flakes, poppy seeds or za'atar to top the bagels.

KEEPING Store bagels, wrapped in plastic wrap, in the fridge for up to 2 days or freeze for up to 3 months.

PREP + COOK TIME 50 MINUTES (+ STANDING) **MAKES** 10

Bagel FLAVOURS & VARIATIONS

EVERYTHING BAGEL

PREP + COOK TIME 50 MINUTES (+ STANDING) **MAKES** 10

Combine 2 tsp poppy seeds in a bowl with 1 tbsp each sesame seeds, dried onion flakes, fennel seeds (or caraway seeds) and linseeds (flaxseeds), and 1 tsp flaked sea salt. Make bagels using recipe on page 32, scattering generously with the seed mixture in step 6. Bake as directed.

SMOKY TOMATO

PREP + COOK TIME 50 MINUTES (+ STANDING) **MAKES** 10

Make bagels using recipe on page 32, adding 1 tsp smoked paprika with the sifted flour in step 1, and reducing milk by ¼ cup and instead adding ¼ cup tomato paste with the rest of the wet ingredients in step 2. Continue as directed in the recipe, scattering bagels with combined 1 tsp each chilli flakes and sea salt flakes instead of seeds in step 6. Bake as directed.

CHEESE & ONION PLEASE

PREP + COOK TIME 50 MINUTES (+ STANDING) **MAKES** 10

Make bagels using recipe on page 32, adding 2 tbsp grated parmesan and 2 tbsp fried shallots after the flour in step 2. Continue as directed in the recipe, scattering bagels with 2 tbsp each fried shallots and grated parmesan instead of seeds in step 6. Bake as directed.

CINNAMON & RAISIN CRUNCH

PREP + COOK TIME 50 MINUTES (+ STANDING) **MAKES** 10

Make bagels using recipe on page 32, adding 2 tsp ground cinnamon with sifted flour in step 1, then mix in ½ cup coarsely chopped raisins and 1 tsp finely grated orange rind after the flour in step 2. Continue as directed in the recipe, scattering bagels with 2 tbsp demerara sugar instead of seeds in step 6. Bake as directed.

Good with... A CREAMY BRIE OR CAMEMBERT CHEESE, HONEYCOMB AND A CRACK OF FRESHLY GROUND BLACK PEPPER, OR WITH SLICED TOMATOES, SMASHED AVOCADO OR HUMMUS OR OTHER GLUTEN-FREE DIPS AND SPREADS.

Sesame tahini CRACKERS

1 Preheat oven to 180°C/350°F. Oil an oven tray; line with baking paper.

2 Place tahini, butter, egg, miso, sesame seeds, a pinch sea salt and the flour in a medium bowl; stir until well combined. Gather mixture together with hands.

3 Roll mixture between sheets of baking paper to a 23cm x 33cm (9in x 13¼in) rectangle. Remove top sheet of paper; trim edges to neaten to 22cm x 32cm (8¾in x 12¾in). Cut dough into eight 8cm x 11cm (3¼in x 4½in) rectangular crackers. Place on tray 2cm (¾in) apart.

4 Bake for 12 minutes or until crisp and golden; the edges will brown faster than the middle. Cool on trays.

KEEPING Crackers will keep in an airtight container in a cool dry place for up to 1 week.

PREP + COOK TIME 35 MINUTES **MAKES** 8

½ cup (140g) hulled tahini, at room temperature
40g (1½oz) butter or coconut oil, melted
2 eggs, beaten lightly
1 tablespoon gluten-free miso or wholegrain mustard
⅓ cup (50g) sesame seeds
½ cup (80g) coconut flour

NUT FREE

Chelsea BUNS

NUT FREE

1¼ cups (310ml) lukewarm milk
2 teaspoons (7g) dried yeast
2 tablespoons caster (superfine) sugar
3½ cups (470g) gluten-free plain (all-purpose) flour
2 teaspoons gluten-free baking powder
¾ teaspoon fine sea salt
1 teaspoon mixed spice
80g (2½oz) butter, melted
1 egg, beaten lightly
1 tablespoon finely grated lemon rind
40g (1½oz) butter, softened
2 tablespoons firmly packed brown sugar
½ cup (80g) currants
¼ teaspoon ground cinnamon

GLACÉ ICING

¾ cup (120g) gluten-free icing (confectioners') sugar
3 teaspoons lemon juice

1 Combine milk, yeast and caster sugar in a bowl. Stand for 10 minutes until foamy.

2 Meanwhile, sift flour, baking powder, salt and mixed spice into a bowl. Add yeast mixture, melted butter, egg and 3 teaspoons of the lemon rind; stir to form a soft dough.

3 Place dough in a large oiled bowl; cover with plastic wrap. Stand in a warm place for 1½ hours until dough almost doubles in size.

4 Grease a 23cm (9¼in) square cake pan. Line base and sides with baking paper (there is no need to extend the paper over the edge).

5 Turn dough out onto a 30cm x 50cm (12in x 20in) piece of baking paper. Place another piece of paper the same size on top. Roll dough out between baking paper into a 30cm x 40cm (12in x 16in) rectangle. Remove top paper.

6 Position dough with the long side in front of you. Spread dough with softened butter, leaving a 2cm (¾in) border on the opposite long side. Scatter with brown sugar and currants. Using the baking paper as an aid, roll up dough from longest side as tightly as possible into a log. Cut into 12 equal-sized pieces. Arrange slices, cut-side up in pan; cover with oiled plastic wrap. Stand in a warm place for 1 hour or until almost doubled in size.

7 Meanwhile, preheat oven to 200°C/400°F.

8 Bake buns for 25 minutes or until golden brown and they sound hollow when tapped. Transfer to a wire rack to cool.

9 Make glacé icing. Drizzle icing over buns; sprinkle with remaining 1 teaspoon lemon rind and the cinnamon.

glacé icing Sift icing sugar into a small heatproof bowl; stir in enough of the lemon juice to make a thick paste. Place bowl over a small saucepan of simmering water; stir until icing is a pouring consistency (do not overheat).

PREP + COOK TIME 50 MINUTES (+ STANDING) **MAKES** 12

STORE BREAD IN AN AIRTIGHT CONTAINER FOR UP TO 3 DAYS OR FREEZE FOR UP TO 1 MONTH.

You need... BANANAS IN TWO STAGES OF RIPENESS FOR THIS RECIPE; SUPER RIPE FOR A FLAVOURSOME BREAD, AND JUST RIPE FOR THE TOP. SERVE SLICES SPREAD THICKLY WTIH BUTTER AND HONEYCOMB.

Banana BREAD

NUT FREE

125g (4oz) butter, softened
⅔ cup (150g) firmly packed brown sugar
1 teaspoon vanilla extract
2 eggs
1 cup (280g) mashed ripe banana
1½ cups (200g) gluten-free self-raising flour
1 teaspoon gluten-free baking powder
1 teaspoon ground cinnamon
½ cup (50g) milk powder
½ cup (125ml) milk or nut-milk
1 medium banana (200g), halved lengthways
1 tablespoon demerara sugar

1 Preheat oven to 180°C/350°F. Grease an 11cm x 30cm (4½in x 12in) loaf pan (top measurement); double line base and sides with baking paper, extending the papers 2cm (¾in) over the sides.

2 Beat butter, brown sugar and vanilla in a medium bowl with an electric mixer until light and creamy. Beat in eggs one at a time. Stir in banana and combined sifted flour, baking powder, cinnamon and milk powder, alternately with the milk. Spoon the batter into the pan; level the surface.

3 Bake loaf for 15 minutes. Remove from oven. Place banana halves on top of loaf, cut-side up, then sprinkle with demerara sugar. Quickly return to oven and bake for a further 45 minutes or until a skewer inserted into the centre comes out clean.

4 Leave loaf in pan for 10 minutes, before turning, top-side up, onto a wire rack to cool. Serve sliced, warm or room temperature.

TIP You will need about 2 ripe bananas to yield 1 cup mashed banana.

PREP + COOK TIME 1 HOUR 15 MINUTES **MAKES** 1 LOAF (15 SLICES)

Good for... BREAKFAST TOASTED WITH SMASHED AVOCADO AND FETTA, FOR LUNCH BOXES WITH YOUR FAVOURITE SANDWICH FILLING OR DINNER AS THE SOFT MOREISH BURGER BUN FOR THE PERFECT HAMBURGER.

Milk bun PULL-APART

8 eggs
3 cups (300g) milk powder
4 teaspoons gluten-free baking powder
1 teaspoon fine sea salt
¼ cup (35g) gluten-free plain (all-purpose) flour

1 Preheat oven to 170°C/340°F. Line a 20cm x 30cm (8in x 12in) slice pan with baking paper.

2 Place eggs in a medium bowl, beat lightly with a fork. Add remaining ingredients. Using a spoon, stir until the mixture forms a smooth, very wet dough. Leave dough for 10 minutes to firm.

3 Form ⅓ cupfuls of the mixture into balls, using wet hands. Arrange balls in tin, in rows of three across and four down.

4 Bake buns for 22 minutes, rotating the pan in the oven halfway through cooking time. Serve warm.

NUT FREE

KEEPING Buns are best eaten on day they are baked or freeze for up to 1 month.

PREP + COOK TIME 45 MINUTES (+ STANDING) **MAKES** 12

TARTS & PIES

You can... SWAP 1 CUP FRESH GLUTEN-FREE BREADCRUMBS FOR ¾ CUP OF STORE-BOUGHT DRY GLUTEN-FREE BREADCRUMBS, IF PREFERRED.

Thai chicken SAUSAGE ROLLS

5 kaffir lime leaves
500g (1lb) minced (ground) chicken
⅓ cup (100g) nut-free green thai curry paste
6 green onions (scallions), chopped finely
½ cup finely chopped coriander (cilantro) leaves and stems
1 cup (100g) fresh gluten-free breadcrumbs
1 tablespoon fish sauce
1 egg yolk
1 tablespoon black or white sesame seeds
¼ cup (70g) sweet chilli sauce
1½ tablespoons lime juice

FLAKY PASTRY
¼ cup (35g) arrowroot flour
¼ cup (45g) rice flour
1¾ cups (235g) gluten-free plain (all-purpose) flour
½ teaspoon fine sea salt
250g (8oz) butter, frozen

1 Make flaky pastry.
2 Preheat oven to 220°C/425°F. Line a large oven tray with baking paper.
3 Cut out the centre vein from lime leaves then slice leaves as finely as possible. Reserve 1 sliced leaf for dipping sauce. Process remaining sliced leaves with chicken, curry paste, green onion, coriander leaves and stems, breadcrumbs and fish sauce until well combined. Transfer to a large bowl.
4 Cut pastry into half. Roll halves out between two sheets of baking paper to 3mm (⅛in) thick and 27cm (10¾in) square. Cut each sheet of pastry in half to form four large rectangles of pastry 13.5cm x 27cm (5½in x 10¾in). Divide the chicken mixture into four and spread along one edge of each pastry rectangle. Lightly brush edge with combined egg yolk and 1 tablespoon chilled water; roll up to enclose, pressing edges to seal. Cut eight diagonal slashes crossways along each sausage roll. Brush with egg yolk mixture; sprinkle with sesame seeds.
5 Place sausage rolls on lined tray; bake for 30 minutes or until browned and chicken is cooked through.
6 Meanwhile, to make the dipping sauce, combine reserved lime leaf, the chilli sauce and lime juice in a small bowl.
7 Cut sausage rolls on the diagonal; serve warm or room temperature with the dipping sauce.

flaky pastry Sift flours and salt into a large bowl; coarsely grate over frozen butter. Using fingertips, rub butter into flour to separate strands. Gradually add ⅔ cup (160ml) chilled water, mixing with a flat-bladed knife until mixture just comes together. Transfer dough to a lightly gluten-free floured surface and shape into a flat disc. Enclose in plastic wrap; refrigerate for 1 hour before using.

KEEPING Sausage rolls are best eaten on the day they are baked or freeze uncooked for up to 1 month. Cook from frozen.

PREP + COOK TIME 55 MINUTES **MAKES** 12

NUT FREE

You can... USE STORE-BOUGHT GLUTEN-FREE PUFF PASTRY AVAILABLE FROM SUPERMARKETS, IF YOU PREFER INSTEAD OF MAKING YOUR OWN PASTRY. PERFECT FOR DINNER WITH STEAMED GREEN BEANS AND OVEN-BAKED CHIPS.

Lamb & rosemary PIES

1 tablespoon extra virgin olive oil
800g (1½lb) boneless lamb shoulder, cut into 2cm (¾in) pieces
2 medium onions (300g), chopped finely
1 clove garlic, crushed
2 sprigs rosemary, plus extra to serve
2 tablespoons tomato paste
1 tablespoon dijon mustard
2½ cups (625ml) gluten-free chicken stock
2 tablespoons 100% corn (maize) cornflour (cornstarch)
1 cup (120g) frozen peas, thawed

GLUTEN-FREE PASTRY
2¾ cups (375g) gluten-free pastry flour
125g (4oz) cold butter, chopped
2 tablespoons tamari
2 tablespoons extra virgin olive oil

1 Heat oil in a medium saucepan over high heat; cook lamb, in batches, turning, for 5 minutes or until browned. Remove from pan.
2 Reduce heat to medium; cook onion and garlic in same pan, stirring, for 5 minutes or until onion is soft. Return lamb to pan with rosemary and combined paste, mustard and chicken stock; bring to the boil. Reduce heat to low; cook, stirring occasionally, for 1½ hours or until lamb is tender and sauce thickens.
3 Combine cornflour and 2 tablespoons water, add to lamb mixture with peas; cook, stirring, over high heat, for 5 minutes or until sauce boils and thickens. Season, cool.
4 Meanwhile, make gluten-free pastry.
5 Preheat oven to 220°C/425°F. Oil six 10cm (4in), ¾ cup (180ml) pie tins; place on an oven tray.
6 Roll pastry between two sheets of baking paper until 4mm (⅛in) thick. Cut six 15cm (6in) rounds from pastry. Ease pastry rounds into tins; press into base and sides, trim edges.
7 Spoon lamb mixture into pastry cases. Brush edges with water. Cut six 10cm (4in) rounds from remaining pastry; place on pies, pressing to seal. Trim edges. Refrigerate for 30 minutes.
8 Make two small cuts into the top of each pie, scatter with extra rosemary and salt. Bake pies for 30 minutes or until tops are firm, browned lightly and filling is hot.

gluten-free pastry Process flour and butter in a food processor until mixture resembles coarse crumbs. With machine operating, gradually pour in combined tamari, oil and ⅔ cup (160ml) water until mixture just comes together. Lightly knead on a surface dusted with a little gluten-free flour into a ball.

KEEPING Freeze pies for up to 3 months; reheat from frozen in a 180°C/350°F oven for 30 minutes or until pies are heated through.

PREP + COOK TIME 2 HOURS 30 MINUTES (+ REFRIGERATION) **MAKES** 6

EGG FREE

You need... POTATO FLOUR FOR THIS RECIPE. IT IS DERIVED BY COOKING AND DEHYDRATING POTATO. IT DIFFERS FROM POTATO STARCH WHICH IS MADE BY EXTRACTING THE STARCH AND IS USED AS A THICKENER.

Cheese TWISTS

250g (8oz) butter, cut into 1cm (½in) cubes
1 cup (160g) brown rice flour
¾ cup (110g) potato flour
½ cup (60g) 100% corn (maize) cornflour (cornstarch)
1 teaspoon sea salt flakes
2 teaspoons xanthan gum
⅓ cup (95g) wholegrain mustard
¾ cup (60g) grated parmesan

NUT FREE

1 Freeze butter cubes for 15 minutes. Line three large oven trays with baking paper.
2 Place flours, salt and xanthan gum in a food processor. Pulse to combine. Add ¾ cup (180ml) chilled water in a steady stream, while pulsing 5 times. Add frozen butter; pulse 5 times, until incorporated but with chunks of butter still quite visible.
3 Turn mixture onto a work surface and push pastry together to form a rectangle. Transfer to a large piece of baking paper. Roll out pastry to a 20cm x 40cm (8in x 16in) rectangle. Pastry will be very crumbly at this stage. Place the short side in front of you. Using the paper to assist you, fold dough into thirds by bringing the top third down over the middle third, then the bottom third up to cover the folded dough. Repeat the rolling out and folding process twice more with dough; enclose in plastic wrap. Refrigerate for 15 minutes.
4 Cut pastry in half crossways; roll each portion out to a 20cm x 30cm (8in x 12in) rectangle between sheets of baking paper. Refrigerate for 30 minutes. Trim the sides. Cut pastry lengthways into 2cm (¾in) wide strips (each strip of pastry should be 2cm (¾in) wide and 30cm (12in) long).
5 Divide mustard between sheets of pastry then spread to cover. Sprinkle with parmesan. Lightly roll over cheese with a rolling pin so it sticks to the pastry. Turn onto a fresh piece of baking paper and remove bottom baking paper so it will not be stuck when removing the strips of pastry. Refrigerate for 30 minutes.
6 Remove each strip of pastry and twist gently; place on trays. Freeze for 1 hour.
7 Preheat oven to 180°C/350°F.
8 Bake twists from frozen for 18 minutes, swapping trays around half way through cooking time if needed. Serve topped with extra grated parmesan, if you like.

KEEPING Twists will keep in an airtight container for up to 3 days or uncooked twists can be frozen for up to 2 months. Cook from frozen.

PREP + COOK TIME 1 HOUR (+ REFRIGERATION & FREEZING) **MAKES** 20

You can... MAKE A SPINACH AND RICOTTA VERSION OF THIS RECIPE. COOK OFF ONION AND GARLIC AS PER THE RECIPE. ADD 2 CUPS BABY SPINACH; COOK UNTIL WILTED. COOL. COMBINE WITH 250G (8OZ) FIRM RICOTTA.

DAIRY FREE

Lamb & pine nut PASTIZZIS

1 Make basic gluten-free fillo pastry on page 71.

2 Preheat oven to 220°C/425°F.

3 Heat oil in a large frying pan over high heat; cook onion, garlic, ginger and spices for 5 minutes or until onion is soft. Add lamb mince; cook, stirring, for 5 minutes or until lamb is cooked through. Add yoghurt; cook, stirring, for 2 minutes or until thickened. Stir in pine nuts, parsley and lemon rind.

4 Using ¼ of the dough, roll pastry out on a large floured piece of baking paper using a well-floured rolling pin until dough is about 1mm thick. Cut dough into 18 x 10cm (4in) rounds. Place a heaped teaspoon of mince mixture on each round; brush edges with egg yolk lightly beaten with milk. Pin and twist the edges together. Place on a baking-paper-lined oven tray; brush with a little more egg mixture.

5 Bake pastizzis for 20 minutes or until crisp and golden.

PREP + COOK TIME 1 HOUR 30 MINUTES **MAKES** 18

1 quantity basic gluten-free fillo pastry (page 71)
2 teaspoons extra virgin olive oil
½ small onion (40g), chopped finely
1 clove garlic, crushed
½ teaspoon grated fresh ginger
½ teaspoon ground cumin
½ teaspoon ground coriander
250g (8oz) minced (ground) lamb
1 tablespoon coconut or greek yoghurt
2 teaspoons toasted pine nuts
1 tablespoon chopped flat-leaf parsley
1 teaspoon finely grated lemon rind
1 egg yolk
1 tablespoon almond or dairy milk

EGG FREE
DAIRY FREE
NUT FREE

PUMPKIN & KALE TART

with tahini cream

1 Preheat oven 200°C/400°F. Line two large oven trays with baking paper.

2 Remove the skin from half the pumpkin. Cut peeled and unpeeled pumpkin into 2cm (¾in) pieces; place on one of the oven trays keeping them separated. Drizzle pumpkin with 1 tablespoon of the oil; season. Roast for 45 minutes or until tender and slightly charred. Place kale on second oven tray, rub in remaining oil; bake alongside pumpkin for the last 10 minutes of cooking time. Reduce oven to 180°C/350°F.

3 Make sesame pastry.

4 Oil two large oven trays. Roll each piece of pastry between sheets of baking paper to make a 5mm (¼in) thick, 15cm x 30cm (6in x 12in) rectangle, trimming edges if necessary. Discard top sheet of baking paper. Transfer pastry with bottom sheet of paper onto each tray. Bake for 12 minutes or until cooked through. Cool.

5 For pumpkin tahini cream, blend or process skinless pumpkin with tahini, garlic and lemon juice. Season.

6 Divide and spread pumpkin tahini cream over each pastry leaving a 1cm (½in) border; top with remaining pumpkin, kale and pomegranate seeds. Drizzle with molasses, and sprinkle with chilli. Cut tart into large wedges to serve.

sesame pastry Process flours, sesame seeds and salt until combined. With the motor operating, add oil and ½ cup (125ml) water, 1 tablespoon at a time, until mixture forms a ball and comes away from the side. Divide pastry into two pieces.

KEEPING Tart is best eaten on the day it is made.

PREP + COOK TIME 1 HOUR 30 MINUTES (+ REFRIGERATION) **SERVES** 4

1kg (2lb) butternut pumpkin, cut into 2cm (¾in) pieces
2 tablespoons extra virgin olive oil
2 cups torn kale leaves
2 tablespoons tahini
1 small clove garlic, crushed
2 tablespoons lemon juice
2 tablespoons pomegranate seeds
1 tablespoon pomegranate molasses
1 long red chilli, sliced thinly

SESAME PASTRY
2 cups (300g) chickpea (besan) flour
½ cup (80g) brown rice flour
⅓ cup (50g) sesame seeds
2 teaspoons sea salt flakes
⅓ cup (80ml) olive oil

You can... ADD A FLAVOUR TWIST TO THE SAUSAGE ROLLS BY USING ONE OF THE FOUR TOPPINGS ON THE FOLLOWING PAGES, OR SIMPLY SPRINKLE WITH A LITTLE FLAKED SEA SALT AND FRESHLY GROUND BLACK PEPPER.

Sausage ROLLS

NUT FREE

2 teaspoons olive oil
1 small leek (200g), white part only, chopped finely
1 small carrot (70g), grated finely
1 clove garlic, crushed
500g (1lb) gluten-free sausage mince
½ teaspoon gluten-free roast lamb seasoning
1 tablespoon tomato paste
1 egg, beaten lightly

GLUTEN-FREE PASTRY
2¾ cups (375g) gluten-free pastry flour
125g (4oz) cold butter, chopped

1 Make gluten-free pastry.

2 Heat oil in a medium frying pan over high heat; cook leek, carrot and garlic, stirring, for 5 minutes or until soft. Cool.

3 Combine mince, seasoning, paste and vegetable mixture in a medium bowl; season.

4 Roll the pastry between sheets of baking paper to make a 22cm x 45cm (9in x 18in) rectangle; remove top paper. Place filling along the length of the pastry in the centre. Using the paper as an aid, roll pastry over the filling. Brush the unrolled pastry edge with egg. Continue rolling then press the pastry lightly to seal. Cut roll in half. Place rolls, seam-side down, on a baking-paper-lined oven tray. Brush with egg; score each roll at 7.5cm (3in) intervals with a sharp knife. Refrigerate for 30 minutes or until firm.

5 Preheat oven to 180°C/350°F.

6 Bake rolls for 20 minutes or until pastry is browned lightly and filling is cooked through. Cut each roll into 9 before serving.

gluten-free pastry Place pastry flour in a large bowl; rub in butter until mixture resembles coarse breadcrumbs. Mix in ⅔ cup (160ml) chilled water until mixture forms a dough. Lightly knead on a surface dusted with a little gluten-free flour into a ball.

TIPS Pastry is best used straight away. If pastry dries out while you are using it, add a little olive oil to the dough. If preferred, use store-bought gluten-free puff pastry, available from major supermarkets.

KEEPING Sausage rolls are best eaten on the day they are baked or uncooked sausage rolls can be frozen for up to 1 month; cook from frozen.

PREP + COOK TIME 1 HOUR 10 MINUTES (+ REFRIGERATION) **MAKES** 18

SAUSAGE ROLL *toppings*

SPICE-IT-UP

PREP TIME 5 MINUTES **MAKES** 2 TABLESPOONS OR ENOUGH FOR 18 SAUSAGE ROLLS

Combine 2 tsp chilli flakes, 1 tbsp sea salt flakes and 2 tsp smoked paprika in a small bowl. Make sausage rolls following recipe on page 57 to the end of step 4; sprinkle with the spice-it-up mixture before refrigeration. Continue as directed in the recipe.

SEED CRUNCH

PREP TIME 5 MINUTES **MAKES** ½ CUP OR ENOUGH FOR 18 SAUSAGE ROLLS

Combine 2 tbsp sunflower seeds, 2 tbsp pepitas (pumpkin seed kernels), 2 tbsp sesame seeds and 2 tsp salt flakes in a small bowl. Make sausage rolls following recipe on page 57 to the end of step 4; sprinkle with the seed crunch before refrigeration. Continue as directed in the recipe.

ITALIAN SPRINKLES

PREP TIME 5 MINUTES **MAKES** 1 CUP OR ENOUGH FOR 18 SAUSAGE ROLLS

Combine ⅓ cup each finely chopped rosemary, grated parmesan and chopped pine nuts with 2 tsp sea salt flakes in a small bowl. Make sausage rolls following recipe on page 57 to the end of step 4; sprinkle with the italian sprinkles before refrigeration. Continue as directed in the recipe.

CURRY MAGIC

PREP TIME 5 MINUTES **MAKES** 3 TABLESPOONS OR ENOUGH FOR 18 SAUSAGE ROLLS

Combine 1 tbsp curry powder with 2 tsp each of sea salt flakes, nigella seeds, fennel seeds and cumin seeds in a small bowl. Make sausage rolls following recipe on page 57 to the end of step 4; sprinkle with the curry magic before refrigeration. Continue as directed in the recipe.

Good with... A BITTER GREEN SALAD FOR LUNCH OR WARMED WITH A MIX OF BLANCHED BROCCOLINI, STEAMED GREEN BEANS AND ASPARAGUS FOR DINNER. OR PACK WEDGES INTO CONTAINERS FOR AN OFFICE LUNCH OR PICNIC.

Bacon, chive & potato QUICHE

NUT FREE

20g (¾oz) butter, melted
200g (6½oz) kipfler potatoes, peeled
2 teaspoons olive oil
1 medium onion (150g), chopped finely
4 rindless gluten-free bacon slices (260g), chopped coarsely
1 quantity gluten-free shortcrust pastry (see page 76)
3 eggs, beaten lightly
1 cup (250ml) pouring cream
1 cup (240g) firm ricotta
⅓ cup (25g) finely grated parmesan
2 tablespoons finely chopped chives

1 Preheat oven to 180°C/350°F. Grease a 5cm (2in) deep, 24cm (9½in) round loose-basedtart tin with melted butter. (The butter will help the pastry to brown.)

2 Boil, steam or microwave potato until tender; drain. Cut into 1.5cm (¾in) thick slices.

3 Heat oil in a small frying pan over medium heat; cook onion and bacon, stirring for 8 minutes or until onion is soft. Drain on paper towel.

4 Roll pastry between two sheets of baking paper until 5mm (¼in) thick. Ease pastry into pan, pushing together any cracks that might form. Press pastry into side and base of pan; trim edges. Place tart tin on an oven tray. (It is not necessary to blind bake the pastry.)

5 Scatter bacon mixture into pastry case; add potato slices. Whisk eggs, cream and ricotta in a medium jug; season. Pour mixture into pastry case and scatter with ¼ cup of the parmesan.

6 Bake quiche on the lowest shelf in the oven for 1 hour or until set. Serve topped with chives and remaining parmesan.

TIPS You can turn this recipe into six individual quiches. Use store-bought gluten-free shortcrust pastry available from major supermarkets, if preferred.

KEEPING Quiche is best eaten on the day it is made. Reheat any leftovers in the oven to warm.

PREP + COOK TIME 1 HOUR 40 MINUTES **SERVES** 6

Good for... BREAKFAST OR BRUNCH WITH FRIED EGGS. SERVE AS LUNCH OR A PICNIC WITH A SIMPLE GREEN SALAD, OR DINNER WITH CHARRED BROCCOLINI AND GREEN BEANS TOSSED IN A GARLIC DRESSING.

Chicken & shiitake HAND PIES

1 Slice two shiitake; cut remaining shiitake into quarters.

2 Heat oil in a large non-stick saucepan over a medium heat. Add leek, onion, garlic with quartered and dried shiitake; cook, stirring, for 3 minutes or until onions are softened. Stir in chicken and ½ cup (125ml) of the cream; season. Reduce heat to low; cook, covered, for 25 minutes or until chicken is very tender. Add remaining cream, cook, uncovered, for a further 5 minutes or until sauce is thick. Transfer to a bowl; refrigerate until cool.

3 Meanwhile, make shiitake pastry.

4 Preheat oven to 180°C/350°F. Line two large oven trays with baking paper.

5 Roll pastry out on a large piece of baking paper until 4mm (⅛in) thick. Cut out six 18cm (7¼in) rounds, re-rolling pastry scraps as necessary.

6 Place ½ cup of filling in centre of each round; fold over one side of pastry to form a half-moon shape, press pastry edges together to seal. Transfer pies to prepared trays. Brush with beaten egg, top with a piece of sliced shiitake mushroom.

7 Bake hand pies for 40 minutes or until golden and pastry is cooked through. Serve immediately.

shiitake pastry Place mushrooms and chia seeds in a spice grinder or powerful blender, pulse to a fine powder. Place shiitake powder, remaining ingredients and ½ cup (125ml) chilled water in a food processor, pulse until a dough forms. Form dough into a disc; enclose in plastic wrap. Refrigerate for 1 hour.

DO-AHEAD Pastry and filling can be made a day head.

KEEPING Pies are best eaten on day they are baked or uncooked pies can be frozen for up to 1 month. Cook from frozen adding an extra 10 minutes to cooking time.

PREP + COOK TIME 1 HOUR 35 MINUTES (+ COOLING) **MAKES** 6

- 125g (4oz) fresh shiitake mushrooms
- 1 tablespoon extra virgin olive oil
- 1 medium leek (350g), white part only, sliced thinly
- 2 green onions (scallions), trimmed, sliced thinly
- 2 cloves garlic, crushed
- 3 dried shiitake mushrooms (10g), torn into chunks
- 4 chicken thigh fillets (680g), cut into 1.5cm (¾in) pieces
- ¾ cup (180ml) thickened (heavy) cream
- 1 egg, beaten lightly

SHIITAKE PASTRY

- 2 dried shiitake mushrooms (10g)
- 2 tablespoons white chia seeds
- 3 cups (405g) gluten-free plain (all-purpose) flour
- ¾ cup (180ml) olive oil
- 60g (2oz) butter, chopped, chilled
- 1 egg

NUT FREE

NUT FREE

You can... ADD A BUNCH OF CHOPPED BROCCOLINI TO THE PIE FILLING AT THE END OF STEP 2 INSTEAD OF THE KALE, IF YOU LIKE. CHOOSE A SPRINKLE TOPPING FROM THE SAUSAGE ROLL SPRINKLES ON PAGE 59, INSTEAD OF THE SESAME SEEDS.

Smoky chicken & corn PIE

2 cups (500ml) gluten-free chicken stock
625g (1¼lb) chicken breast fillets
60g (2oz) butter
1 small leek (200g), sliced thinly
2 cobs trimmed corn (500g), kernels removed
1 teaspoon smoked paprika
2 tablespoons 100% corn (maize) cornflour (cornstarch)
½ cup (125ml) milk
1 cup (250ml) pouring cream
2 cups (100g) torn kale leaves
1 quantity gluten-free shortcrust pastry (see page 76)
1 egg yolk, beaten with 1 teaspoon water
1 tablespoon sesame seeds

1 Bring stock to the boil in a medium saucepan over high heat. Add chicken; return to the boil. Reduce heat, simmer, covered, for 10 minutes or until chicken is cooked. Remove from heat; stand chicken in poaching liquid for 10 minutes. Remove chicken; chop coarsely. Reserve 1 cup of the poaching liquid; keep remaining liquid for another use, or discard.

2 Heat butter in a medium saucepan over medium heat; cook leek and corn, stirring for 5 minutes or until softened. Add paprika, cook, stirring, for 1 minute. Combine reserved poaching liquid and cornflour in a jug. Stir into leek mixture, with milk and cream. Cook, stirring, until mixture boils and thickens. Stir in chopped chicken and kale. Season to taste. Cool for 15 minutes.

3 Preheat oven to 200°C/400°F. Grease a 22cm x 30cm (9in x 12¾in) oval 2-litre (8-cup) ovenproof dish.

4 Roll the pastry between two sheets of baking paper to make a 5mm (¼in) thick, 35cm x 40cm (14in x 16in) rectangle. Cut pastry crossways into 5cm (2in) wide strips.

5 Spoon chicken mixture into ovenproof dish; place pastry strips crossways, slightly overlapping each other, over pie filling. Press edges to side of dish; trim excess. Brush pastry with egg yolk mixture; sprinkle with sesame seeds. Make a small cut in the centre of the pastry.

6 Bake pie for 35 minutes or until golden brown and filling is heated through.

KEEPING Pie is best eaten on the day it is made.

PREP + COOK TIME 1 HOUR **SERVES** 6

Deep-dish almond APPLE PIE

1 Process almond meal, flours, 2 tablespoons of the sugar, xanthan gum, salt and butter until mixture resembles breadcrumbs. Gradually add ¼ cup (60ml) chilled water; process until mixture just comes together. Gently knead dough on a lightly gluten-free floured surface until smooth. Divide dough in half and shape each into a disc; refrigerate for 30 minutes or until firm.

2 Meanwhile, make filling.

3 Preheat oven to 180°C/350°F. Lightly grease a 24cm (9½in) round, 3cm (1¼in) deep pie tin.

4 Roll out each pastry portion between two sheets of baking paper into a 30cm (12in) round. Lift onto a tray; refrigerate for 10 minutes to firm. Line pie dish with pastry round. Cut remaining rolled pastry into 4cm (1½in) wide strips. Spoon filling into pie case. Arrange pastry strips in a lattice pattern over filling. Trim pastry edge; reserving scraps if needed to re-roll pastry to complete lattice pattern. Brush lattice with egg; scatter with remaining sugar. Wipe rim clean. Transfer pie to an oven tray.

5 Bake pie for 45 minutes, on the lowest oven shelf, covering with foil if overbrowning. Leave pie in tin for 10 minutes before transferring to a wire rack to cool completely. Serve with gluten-free vanilla ice-cream, if you like.

filling Combine apple, sugar, ½ cup (125ml) water, juice and spices in a medium saucepan. Stir over low heat until sugar dissolves; bring to a simmer. Cook, covered, for 6 minutes or until apples are just tender and still hold their shape well. Using a slotted spoon, spoon apples into a bowl. Bring syrup in saucepan to simmer; cook for 3 minutes or until reduced. Pour syrup over apples in bowl; mix well and cool.

KEEPING Pie is best eaten on the day it is baked or freeze uncooked pie for up to 1 month. Cook from frozen, adding 5 minutes to the cooking time. Any leftovers can be reheated in the oven for 20 minutes.

PREP + COOK TIME 1 HOUR 55 MINUTES (+ REFRIGERATION) **SERVES** 6

1½ cups (180g) almond meal
1 cup (180g) rice flour
¾ cup (1150g) arrowroot flour
⅓ cup (75g) raw caster (superfine) sugar
3 teaspoons xanthan gum
¼ teaspoon fine sea salt
200g (6½oz) cold butter, chopped
1 egg, beaten lightly

FILLING

1kg (2lb) granny smith apples, peeled, cored, cut into 1cm (½in) thick slices
½ cup (110g) raw caster (superfine) sugar
¼ cup (60ml) lemon juice
2 teaspoons ground cinnamon
½ teaspoon ground nutmeg

You can... ALSO MAKE ONE LARGE GALETTE; ROLL PASTRY TO A 30CM X 40CM RECTANGLE. SPOON OVER MARMALADE, LEAVING A 6CM BORDER, TOP WITH FRUIT. FOLD IN BORDER TO FORM RUSTIC CRUST. CONTINUE RECIPE AS DIRECTED.

Plum, hazelnut & ginger GALETTES

1 Process hazelnut meal, rice flour, icing sugar, cinnamon, butter, and 3 lightly beaten eggs until mixture forms a ball. Shape dough into four discs; enclose each in plastic wrap. Refrigerate for 30 minutes.

2 Meanwhile, preheat oven to 160°C/325°F. Grease a large oven tray.

3 Halve and stone plums, then slice crossways in 3mm (⅛in) thin slices; toss plums, caster sugar, and arrowroot together in a large bowl. Stand for 20 minutes to soften plums slightly.

4 Roll each disc of pastry out between two sheets of baking paper to make a 20cm (8in) round. Transfer pastry on paper to oven tray. Remove the top sheet of paper and discard. Spoon marmalade over pastry, leaving a 6cm (2½in) border. Arrange plums over marmalade overlapping slices slightly. Using the paper as an aid, fold in the pastry border, pleating it as you go to form a 3cm (1¼in) rustic crust. Press down lightly to secure edge. Pour any plum juices in bowl into the centre of the galettes. Lightly beat remaining egg, brush over pastry edges; sprinkle edges with demerara sugar.

5 Bake galettes on the top shelf of the oven for 40 minutes or until pastry is golden, cooked through, and plums have softened. Cool galettes on tray for 10 minutes. Serve with ice-cream.

KEEPING Galettes are best eaten on the day they are made.

PREP + COOK TIME 1 HOUR 45 MINUTES (+ REFRIGERATION) **MAKES** 4

3½ cups (350g) hazelnut meal
⅔ cup (120g) rice flour
¼ cup (40g) gluten-free icing (confectioners') sugar
½ teaspoon ground cinnamon
50g (1½oz) cold unsalted butter
4 eggs
6 blood plums (510g)
2 tablespoons raw sugar
3 teaspoons arrowroot flour
½ cup (160g) ginger marmalade
2 tablespoons demerara sugar
gluten-free vanilla ice-cream, to serve

1/2 CUP
125 ml

DAIRY FREE

You can... USE THIS FILLO PASTRY TO MAKE THE PASTIZZIS ON PAGE 53 OR FOR ANY OF YOUR OTHER FAVOURITE RECIPES THAT USE FILLO PASTRY. OR SIMPLY IMPROVISE AND USE FRIDGE LEFTOVERS TO MAKE FREE-FORM PIES.

Gluten-free FILLO PASTRY

3⅔ cups (495g) gluten-free plain (all-purpose) flour
1 tablespoon xanthan gum
2 teaspoons table salt
125g (4oz) dairy-free spread

1 Process flour, 1½ cups (375ml) water, xanthan gum, salt and dairy-free spread until mixture comes together. Turn onto a lightly gluten-free-floured surface; knead lightly until smooth.

2 Divide dough into four portions. Enclose each portion in plastic wrap.

3 Using one portion of the pastry at a time; roll pastry out on a large floured piece of baking paper using a well-floured rolling pin until dough is about 1mm thick.

4 Repeat process with remaining dough as required.

TIP You will need a quarter of the dough for the recipe on page 53.

KEEPING The dough can be made a day ahead. Cover in plastic wrap and leave at room temperature. Dough can be used for tarts and pies. Freeze for up to 2 months.

PREP TIME 1 HOUR **MAKES** 1KG (2LB) OR 24 SHEETS

Good with... CHEAT'S GINGER ICE-CREAM: FOLD 1 CUP FINELY CHOPPED CRYSTALLISED GINGER INTO 1 LITRE SOFTENED GLUTEN-FREE ICE-CREAM. OR FOLD A COUPLE OF TABLESPOONS CHOPPED CRYSTALLISED GINGER THROUGH THICK CREAM OR GREEK YOGHURT TO SERVE ALONGSIDE.

Pear TARTE TARTIN

1 Make flaky pastry.

2 Melt butter and sugar in a large frying pan over medium heat. Add cream; cook, stirring, until sugar dissolves. Bring to the boil. Add pears in a single layer; reduce heat to low, simmer, turning occasionally, for 20 minutes or until tender.

3 Preheat oven to 240°C/475°F. Lightly grease a 27cm (10¾in) ovenproof frying pan.

4 Remove pears from caramel, place cut-side down, into lined pan in a single layer leaving 1cm (½in) border between pan and pears. Pour caramel over pears.

5 Roll pastry out between two sheets of baking paper to 4mm (⅙in) thick. Remove top paper. Cut out a 29cm (11¾in) round using a plate or large bowl as a guide. Remove pastry scraps around round. Flip pastry onto pears. Remove baking paper; tuck pastry between pears and side of pan.

6 Bake tart for 35 minutes or until pastry is browned and puffed. Cool for 5 minutes, then turn tart onto a platter.

flaky pastry Sift flours into a large bowl; coarsely grate butter over flour. Using your fingertips, rub butter strands into flour. Gradually add ⅔ cup (160ml) chilled water, mixing with a flat-bladed knife until mixture just comes together. Transfer dough to a lightly gluten-free floured surface; shape into a disc. Enclose in plastic wrap; refrigerate for 1 hour before using.

KEEPING Tarte tartin is best eaten on the day it is made.

PREP + COOK TIME 1 HOUR 35 MINUTES **SERVES** 8

50g (1½oz) butter
¾ cup (165g) firmly packed brown sugar
⅔ cup (160ml) thickened (heavy) cream
4 large pears (800g), halved

FLAKY PASTRY
¼ cup (35g) arrowroot flour
¼ cup (45g) rice flour
1¾ cups (235g) gluten-free plain (all-purpose) flour
250g (8oz) butter, frozen

NUT FREE

You can... SWAP PEACHES WITH HALVED APRICOTS IN EARLY SUMMER, NECTARINES IN MID-SUMMER, OR BLOOD PLUMS IN AUTUMN, OR, FOR A TUTTI-FRUTTI STYLE CRUMBLE TART, TRY A MIX OF STONE FRUIT.

Peach & sour cream
CRUMBLE TART

1 Make sweet shortcrust pastry.

2 Preheat oven to 180°C/350°F.

3 Roll the pastry between two sheets of baking paper to make a 4mm (⅛in) thick, 30cm x 40cm (12in x 16in) oval. Remove top sheet of baking paper. Lift the pastry on paper onto a large oven tray.

4 Make walnut crumble.

5 Toss peaches with sour cream and brown sugar in a large bowl. Scatter half of the walnut crumble over pastry leaving a 4cm (1½in) border. Top crumble with peaches (reserving sour cream mixture in bowl). Using baking paper as an aid, fold up pastry to form a crust. Pour over remaining sour cream mixture and scatter with remaining crumble. Brush pastry crust with egg and scatter with demerara sugar.

6 Bake tart for 50 minutes or until lightly browned and peaches have softened. Stand on oven tray for 15 minutes before serving dusted with icing sugar.

sweet shortcrust pastry Process flour, chia seeds, sugar and butter until mixture is crumbly. Add eggs and ½ cup (125ml) chilled water; process until ingredients just come together. Turn dough onto a gluten-free floured surface, knead gently until smooth. Shape into a disc. Cover with plastic wrap; refrigerate for 30 minutes.

walnut crumble Combine flour, sugar and butter in a medium bowl. Rub in butter until mixture resembles breadcrumbs; mix in walnuts. Press mixture together with your fingertips to form small clusters.

KEEPING Crumble tart is best eaten on the day it is made.

PREP + COOK TIME 1 HOUR (+ REFRIGERATION & STANDING)
SERVES 12

6 small peaches (690g), cut into wedges
250g (8oz) sour cream
½ cup (110g) firmly packed brown sugar
1 egg, beaten lightly
2 tablespoons demerara sugar
gluten-free icing (confectioners') sugar, to dust

SWEET SHORTCRUST PASTRY
3½ cups (470g) gluten-free plain (all-purpose) flour
2 tablespoons white chia seeds
2 tablespoons caster (superfine) sugar
160g (5oz) cold butter, chopped
2 eggs

WALNUT CRUMBLE
¾ cup (100g) gluten-free plain (all-purpose) flour
⅓ cup (75g) firmly packed brown sugar
75g (2½oz) cold butter, diced
½ cup (50g) walnuts

Gluten-free shortcrust PASTRY

1 Place pastry mix in a large bowl; rub in butter with your fingers until mixture resembles coarse breadcrumbs. Combine ⅔ cup (160ml) water, tamari and oil in a jug. Using a flat-bladed knife, 'cut' wet ingredients through dry ingredients until mixture forms a dough. Lightly knead dough on a surface dusted with a little gluten-free flour into a ball.

2 Roll pastry between two sheets of baking paper until 5mm (¼in) thick. Use this pastry for any of your favourite savoury recipes that use a shortcrust pastry.

TIPS Pastry is best used immediately. Rolling the pastry between sheets of baking paper will prevent the dough from sticking to the bench. If pastry dries out while you are using it, add a little more olive oil to the dough. If pastry cracks when you are rolling it out or placing it into tart cases etc., it can quickly and easily be pushed back together without ruining it.

KEEPING Pastry is best made close to using.

PREP TIME 10 MINUTES **MAKES** 640G (1¼LB) SHORTCRUST PASTRY

375g (12oz) packet gluten-free pastry mix
125g (4oz) cold butter, chopped coarsely
2 tablespoons tamari
2 tablespoons olive oil
gluten-free plain (all-purpose) flour, for dusting

EGG FREE

REFINED SUGAR FREE

Pumpkin PIE

1.5kg (3lb) kent pumpkin
4 eggs
½ cup (125ml) pure maple syrup
300ml thickened (heavy) cream
1 teaspoon vanilla extract
1 teaspoon ground cinnamon, plus extra to dust
½ teaspoon ground nutmeg
½ teaspoon ground allspice
½ teaspoon ground ginger
2 tablespoons roasted pecans, chopped coarsely
¼ cup (60ml) pure maple syrup, extra

PECAN PASTRY
¼ cup (40g) brown rice flour
1¼ cups (150g) pecans
2 tablespoons white chia seeds
2 pitted fresh dates (40g), chopped finely
2½ tablespoons pure maple syrup
40g (1½oz) butter, melted

1 Preheat oven to 160°C/325°F. Grease a 24cm (9½in) ceramic or metal pie dish.

2 Make pecan pastry.

3 Increase oven temperature to 180°C/350°F.

4 Cut pumpkin into wedges with skin on; discard seeds. Place pumpkin on a baking-paper-lined oven tray. Bake for 45 minutes or until tender. Cool.

5 Scoop flesh from pumpkin wedges; you will need 3 cups. Process the 3 cups of cooled pumpkin flesh until smooth. Add eggs, one at a time, processing after each addition. Add maple syrup, ½ cup (125ml) cream, vanilla and spices; process until well combined. Pour pumpkin mixture into pastry case.

6 Bake pie for 1 hour or until set, covering the edge of the pastry with baking paper if overbrowning. Cool.

7 Beat remaining cream with an electric mixer until soft peaks form. Serve pie topped with whipped cream, pecans and extra maple syrup; dust with extra cinnamon.

pecan pastry Process flour, pecans and chia seeds until finely ground. Add combined dates, maple syrup and butter; process until mixture forms a ball. Roll out pastry between two sheets of baking paper until 5mm (¼in) thick. Refrigerate pastry for 10 minutes. Peel off top sheet of paper and invert pastry into dish. Carefully remove remaining baking paper; press pastry into base and side of dish, trim edges. Line pastry with baking paper; fill with dried beans or rice. Bake for 20 minutes or until dry around the edge. Remove paper and beans; bake for a further 5 minutes or until pastry case is completely dry, covering edges with foil if over browning.

KEEPING Pie is best eaten on the day it is made.

PREP + COOK TIME 2 HOURS (+ COOLING) **SERVES** 10

Goes with... GLUTEN-FREE ICE-CREAM OR FROZEN YOGHURT, THICK CREAM OR VANILLA BEAN CUSTARD FOR A LUSCIOUS WARMING DESSERT.

Rhubarb & pear PIE

⅔ cup (90g) gluten-free plain (all-purpose) flour
½ cup (80g) coconut flour
⅓ cup (40g) almond meal
2 tablespoons gluten-free icing (confectioners') sugar
125g (4oz) cold butter, chopped
1 egg, beaten lightly
2 tablespoons demerara sugar

RHUBARB & PEAR FILLING
1kg (2lb) rhubarb, chopped
2 packham pears (460g), cut into 2cm (¾in) pieces
½ cup (110g) caster (superfine) sugar
⅓ cup (60g) crystallised ginger, chopped
2 teaspoons vanilla bean paste

1 Preheat oven to 180°C/350°F. Grease a 23cm (9in) ceramic or metal pie dish.
2 Make rhubarb and pear filling.
3 Meanwhile, process flours, almond meal and icing sugar until just combined. Add butter, process until mixture resembles breadcrumbs. Add egg and 1 tablespoon chilled water, process until combined. Tip mixture onto a sheet of plastic wrap, bring together into a disc. Wrap mixture; refrigerate for 15 minutes.
4 Spoon filling into pie dish. Roll pastry between two sheets of baking paper to form a round large enough to cover top of pie dish. Carefully peel top sheet of baking paper from pastry, and using the bottom sheet, invert pastry disc to top pie. Carefully remove baking paper; trim edges. Brush with egg and cut a cross into the centre. Scatter with demerara sugar.
5 Bake pie for 30 minutes or until pastry is crisp and golden. Stand for 10 minutes before serving.

rhubarb & pear filling Preheat oven to 180°C/350°F. Place rhubarb, pear and sugar in a roasting dish; roast for 30 minutes. Transfer rhubarb mixture to a medium saucepan; cook, stirring, over high heat for 5 minutes or until thick. Cool. Stir in ginger and vanilla. Cover; refrigerate until required.

KEEPING Pie is best eaten on the day it is made.

PREP + COOK TIME 50 MINUTES (+ REFRIGERATION) **SERVES** 8

SCONES & MUFFINS

You can… ALSO BAKE THE SCONE LOAVES AS A SLICE IN A BAKING-PAPER-LINED 20CM X 30CM (8IN X 12IN) RECTANGULAR SLICE PAN FOR 25 MINUTES. SERVE LOAVES SLICED FRESH OR TOASTED.

Parmesan corn scone LOAVES

1 Preheat oven to 180°C/350°F. Grease four 7cm x 13.5cm (2¾in x 5½in) loaf pans, line bases with baking paper.

2 Place flour, almond meal, polenta, ½ cup (40g) parmesan, sugar and 2 teaspoons of the salt in a food processor; pulse to combine. Add cold butter; pulse until fine crumbs form.

3 Combine egg whites and buttermilk in a jug. Add to polenta mixture through the top of food processor in a steady stream, while pulsing in bursts, until just combined. Divide mixture into pans; level surface with an offset metal palette knife. Mix 1 egg yolk with a little water and brush over loaves (discard remaining egg yolk). Sprinkle loaves with remaining ¼ cup (20g) parmesan, and combined chilli and remaining salt.

4 Bake scone loaves for 20 minutes, rotating pans in the oven halfway through cooking time. Cool loaves in pans for 5 minutes before transferring, top-side up, to a wire rack to cool slightly.

KEEPING Parmesan corn scone loaves are best eaten on the day they are baked or may be frozen for up to 1 month.

PREP + COOK TIME 35 MINUTES **MAKES** 4 LOAVES (18 SLICES)

1¼ cups (170g) gluten-free self-raising flour
1 cup (120g) almond meal
¾ cup (130g) polenta (cornmeal)
¾ cup (60g) grated parmesan
2 tablespoons caster (superfine) sugar
3 teaspoons sea salt flakes
175g (5½oz) cold butter, chopped
2 eggs, separated
1⅓ cups (330ml) buttermilk
½ teaspoon dried chilli flakes

Good for... BREAKFAST WITH A FRIED EGG, LUNCH WITH RICOTTA, SLICED RIPE TOMATOES AND ROCKET LEAVES, OR FOR DINNER WITH A RICH BEEF STEW OR HEARTY SOUP. FOR A PICNIC, SERVE PILED WITH SLICED LEG HAM AND CHUTNEY OR MUSTARD, OR SERVE AS A SNACK SPREAD WITH GOAT'S OR CREAM CHEESE.

Savoury pumpkin streusel SCONES

500g (1lb) kent pumpkin
3 cups (405g) gluten-free plain (all-purpose) flour
¼ cup (50g) pepitas (pumpkin seed kernels)
3 teaspoons gluten-free baking powder
¼ teaspoon ground nutmeg
1½ tablespoons caster (superfine) sugar
1 teaspoon sea salt flakes
150g (4½oz) cold unsalted butter, chopped
1 egg, separated
¾ cup (180ml) buttermilk

STREUSEL TOPPING
¼ cup (50g) pepitas (pumpkin seed kernels)
2 tablespoons gluten-free plain (all-purpose) flour
25g (¾oz) butter
75g (2½oz) fetta, crumbled

1 Preheat oven to 200°C/400°F. Grease a large oven tray; line with baking paper.

2 Place pumpkin (you should have 400g/12½oz peeled and chopped pumpkin) in a microwave safe bowl and cover with plastic wrap. Microwave on HIGH (100%) for 5 minutes or until pumpkin is tender. Leave covered for a further 5 minutes to steam. Drain any excess liquid then mash with a fork until smooth. Refrigerate for 20 minutes or until cold.

3 Process flour, pepitas, baking powder, nutmeg, sugar, salt and butter in a food processor until mixture resembles fine breadcrumbs. Add egg white, mashed pumpkin and ⅔ cup (160ml) buttermilk; pulse to combine. Transfer to a work surface; knead lightly to form a smooth ball. Roll out to a 26cm (10½in) round; cut into 10 wedges. Transfer wedges together to oven tray.

4 Make streusel topping.

5 Combine remaining 1 tablespoon buttermilk and egg yolk in a bowl; brush over scones. Scatter over streusel mixture.

6 Bake scones on the top third of the oven for 20 minutes or until golden and they sound hollow when tapped. Cool for 10 minutes before serving with extra butter. Sprinkle with fresh thyme leaves, if you like.

streusel topping Coarsely chop pepitas; place in a bowl with flour and butter. Rub in butter with your fingertips until mixture resembles coarse bread crumbs. Stir in fetta.

KEEPING Scones are best made close to serving.

PREP + COOK TIME 1 HOUR 15 MINUTES **SERVES** 10

REFINED SUGAR FREE

You can... MAKE A DOUBLE BATCH OF THESE GENEROUS CAFE-STYLE MUFFINS TO FREEZE IN AIRTIGHT CONTAINERS FOR UP TO 2 MONTHS. SERVE WARM FOR BREAKFAST OR AS A LUNCH BOX OR AFTERNOON SNACK.

Spiced almond TEFF MUFFINS

185g (6oz) butter
¾ cup (165g) coconut sugar
3 eggs
1½ cups (180g) almond meal
1 cup (160g) ivory or dark teff flour
3 teaspoons vanilla bean paste
3 teaspoons gluten-free baking powder
1½ teaspoons ground ginger
¾ cup (180ml) gluten-free ginger beer

1 Preheat oven to 180°C/350°F. Line a 6-hole (½-cup/125ml) muffin pan with paper cases.

2 Beat butter and sugar with an electric mixer for 5 minutes or until light and fluffy. Add one egg at a time, beating well after each addition. With the motor operating, add remaining ingredients, one by one. Beat until smooth.

3 Divide batter evenly among paper cases. Bake for 20 minutes. Cool on a wire rack.

TIP Teff flour and grains are derived from the seeds of a hardy grass, traditionally eaten in Ethiopia. They are available from health food stores, major supermarkets and delis, and are gluten free.

KEEPING Muffins will keep in an airtight container for up to 3 days.

PREP + COOK TIME 30 MINUTES (+ COOLING) **MAKES** 6

NUT FREE

Good for... AFTERNOON TEA WITH A DOLLOP OF THICK CREAM. SERVE A COUPLE FOR A SUPER QUICK DESSERT IN BOWLS TOPPED WITH SCOOPS OF VANILLA BEAN ICE-CREAM OR LASHINGS OF POURING CREAM AND MORE MAPLE SYRUP.

Buttermilk maple syrup SCONES

¾ cup (180ml) pure maple syrup
140g (4½oz) butter, chopped
2 cups (270g) gluten-free self-raising flour
¼ cup (25g) milk powder
1 cup (250ml) buttermilk

1 Preheat oven to 200°C/400°F. Lightly grease a 12-hole (⅓-cup/80ml) muffin pan.

2 Place maple syrup and 60g (2oz) butter in a small saucepan; stir over medium heat until butter melts. Divide between the muffin holes.

3 Sift flour and milk powder into a large bowl; add the remaining chopped butter. Using your fingertips, rub butter into flour mixture until it resembles fine breadcrumbs. Make a well in the centre and gently mix in buttermilk until just combined.

4 Turn dough out onto a lightly gluten-free floured surface; lightly knead to bring together. Roll out until 1.5cm (¾in) thick. Cut dough out using a 6cm (2½in) gluten-free floured cutter and place in each muffin hole, re-rolling scraps as you go.

5 Bake for 12 minutes or until a scone sounds hollow when it is tapped. Turn scones out immediately and serve warm.

KEEPING Scones are best made close to serving.

PREP + COOK TIME 25 MINUTES **MAKES** 12

Good for... PICNICS WITH A LEAFY GREEN SALAD AND LEMONY DRESSING. CUT INTO WEDGES AND SERVE WITH HUMMUS FOR YOUR LUNCH BOX, OR SERVE AS A SUMMER DINNER WITH GRILLED LAMB OR IN WINTER WITH HEARTY SOUPS.

Beetroot & fetta PAN MUFFIN

1 bunch each of red and yellow baby beetroot (beets) (500g)
2 teaspoons extra virgin olive oil
2 cups (270g) gluten-free self-raising flour
2 teaspoons gluten-free baking powder
2 teaspoons finely chopped thyme
200g (6½oz) fetta, crumbled
¾ cup (180ml) milk
125g (4oz) butter, melted
1 egg, beaten lightly
¼ cup (40g) natural seed mix (see tip)

1 Preheat oven to 180°C/350°F. Grease a 26m (10½in) round ovenproof frying pan or 20cm x 30cm (8in x 12in) slice pan; line base and long sides with baking paper, extending paper 2cm (¾in) on each side.

2 Trim and scrub beetroot, keeping a little of the stalks attached. Cut beetroot into thin slices lengthways. Place in a small bowl with oil; toss to coat.

3 Sift flour and baking powder into a medium bowl. Add thyme and half the fetta. Stir in milk, butter and egg to make a soft, sticky dough.

4 Spread mixture into prepared pan. Top with sliced beetroot and remaining fetta; scatter top with seed mix.

5 Bake for 30 minutes or until browned and firm when pressed in the centre.

TIP Natural seed mix is a combination of pepitas (pumpkin seed kernels), sunflower seeds and pine nuts. Serve the pan muffin cut into wedges.

KEEPING Best eaten on the day it is made.

PREP + COOK TIME 45 MINUTES **SERVES** 8

Chocolate, honey & TAHINI TWIST

3 cups (405g) gluten-free plain (all-purpose) flour
⅔ cup (120g) rice flour
½ teaspoon cream of tartar
1 teaspoon xanthan gum
½ teaspoon fine sea salt
3 teaspoons (10g) dried yeast
120g (4oz) butter, softened
1⅓ cups (330ml) milk
¼ cup (90g) honey, plus 2 tablespoons extra
2 egg yolks

HONEY TAHINI FILLING

40g (1½oz) butter, softened slightly
2 tablespoons honey
2 tablespoons tahini
100g (3oz) dark (semi-sweet) chocolate, melted, cooled

1 Make honey tahini filling.

2 Preheat oven to 180°C/350°F. Grease a 7.5cm (3in) deep, 13.5cm x 26cm (5½in x 10½in) loaf pan; line base and sides with baking paper, extending the paper 2cm (¾in) over the sides.

3 Sift flours, cream of tartar, xanthan gum and salt into the large bowl of an electric mixer, fitted with paddle attachment. Combine yeast, 100g (3oz) butter, the milk, honey and egg yolks; add to dry ingredients. Mix on low speed until a smooth dough forms.

4 Transfer dough to a large piece of baking paper, about 60cm (24in) long. Place another piece of baking paper of the same size over dough. Roll into a slightly larger than 40cm x 50cm (16in x 20in) rectangle, then trim square to stated size.

5 Position the dough so a long side is in front of you. Spread filling evenly over dough. Using the paper as an aid, roll into a tight 50cm (20in) long log. Cut dough in half lengthways and twist the two lengths together. Place in the loaf pan, then cover dough with oiled plastic wrap. Stand in a warm place for 1 hour or until risen by a quarter.

6 Place loaf pan onto an oven tray; remove plastic wrap. Bake loaf for 30 minutes or until firm to touch. Leave in pan for 10 minutes before placing, top-side up, on a chopping board.

7 Meanwhile, heat remaining 20g (¾oz) butter and extra honey in a small saucepan over low heat until simmering. Drizzle honey mixture over warm loaf.

honey tahini filling Whisk ingredients until smooth. Refrigerate for 30 minutes or until a spreadable consistency. (Do not refrigerate longer than 30 minutes otherwise it will become too firm to spread.)

KEEPING Tahini twist is best eaten on the day it is made.

PREP + COOK TIME 1 HOUR 15 MINUTES (+ STANDING) **SERVES** 10

You can... ALSO MAKE A VARIATION OF THE SCROLLS WITH THE SAME WEIGHT OF PEARS AS APPLES AND SWAPPING PECANS FOR WALNUTS. TOP SCROLLS WITH A LITTLE DEMERARA SUGAR FOR CRUNCH.

Buckwheat & apple CARAMEL SCROLLS

1 Preheat oven to 180°C/350°F. Grease 10 holes of 2 x 6-hole texas (¾-cup/180ml) muffin pans. Line the bases with baking paper.

2 Sift flours, xanthan gum, cream of tartar and salt into a large bowl of an electric mixer fitted with the paddle attachment. Stir in sugar and yeast. In a jug, combine milk, 100g (3oz) of the softened butter and egg yolks. Add to dry ingredients. Mix on low speed until a smooth firm dough forms.

3 Transfer dough to a 40cm (16in) long piece of baking paper. Place another piece of baking paper over dough and roll out to a 30cm x 40cm (12in x 16in) rectangle.

4 To make apple filling, combine ingredients in a bowl.

5 Position the dough with a long side in front of you. Spread the remaining 60g (2oz) of the softened butter evenly over dough; spoon apple mixture evenly over butter, leaving a 2cm (¾in) border on the opposite long side. Gently press apple mixture into dough. Starting from the long edge, roll dough up firmly into a 40cm (16in) long roll.

6 Using a sharp knife, and without putting too much pressure on the dough, cut dough into 10 x 4cm (1½in) scrolls. Transfer scrolls, cut-side up, to prepared holes. Cover scrolls with oiled plastic warp. Stand in a warm place for 1 hour or until risen by one quarter.

7 Bake scrolls for 30 minutes or until golden and cooked through. Leave in pans for 2 minutes before transferring to a wire rack. Serve scrolls drizzled with warm dulce de leche.

KEEPING Scrolls are best served warm on the day they are made.

PREP + COOK TIME 1 HOUR (+ STANDING) **MAKES** 10

3 cups (405g) gluten-free plain (all-purpose) flour
⅔ cup (100g) buckwheat flour
1 teaspoon xanthan gum
½ teaspoon cream of tartar
½ teaspoon fine sea salt
2 tablespoons raw sugar
3 teaspoons (10g) dried yeast
1⅓ cups (330ml) milk
160g (5oz) butter, softened
2 egg yolks
½ cup (150g) dulce de leche, warmed

APPLE FILLING
2 medium granny smith apples (300g), peeled, cored, chopped finely
¾ cup (165g) raw caster (superfine) sugar
⅓ cup (40g) almond meal
⅔ cup (75g) coarsely chopped walnuts
2 teaspoons ground cinnamon

DAIRY FREE

Good for... NOT ONLY BREAKFAST, BUT ALSO AS A LUNCH BOX OR PICNIC TREAT. YOU CAN MIX THE FLAVOURS UP BY SWAPPING THE ALMOND MEAL FOR HAZELNUT MEAL AND USING MIXED SPICE AND A PINCH OF NUTMEG IN PLACE OF CINNAMON.

Brekkie MUFFINS

1 cup (135g) gluten-free self-raising flour
1 teaspoon ground cinnamon
2 tablespoons black or white chia seeds, plus 2 teaspoons extra
1 cup (100g) almond meal
½ cup (80g) coconut sugar
1 cup (250ml) coconut yoghurt (see tip)
¼ cup (60ml) melted coconut oil
2 eggs, beaten lightly

1 Preheat oven to 190°C/375°F. Line a 6-hole (½-cup/125ml) muffin pan with paper cases.

2 Sift flour and cinnamon into a large bowl; stir in chia seeds, almond meal and sugar. Make a well in the centre. Whisk coconut yoghurt, coconut oil and egg in a large jug. Pour into dry ingredients; stir until just combined. Spoon mixture into paper cases; sprinkle with extra chia seeds.

3 Bake muffins for 25 minutes or until muffins are cooked when a skewer is inserted and comes out clean. Stand muffins in pan for 5 minutes before transferring to a wire rack to cool.

TIPS Serve muffins dolloped with dairy-free spread or butter, and drizzled with honey. If the coconut yoghurt you are using is very thick reduce the amount by 1 tablespoon and add 1 tablespoon water.

KEEPING Muffins are best eaten on the day they are made or eaten warmed up the following day.

PREP + COOK TIME 35 MINUTES **MAKES** 6

Brekkie MUFFIN VARIATIONS

PEACH & COCONUT MUFFINS

PREP + COOK TIME 35 MINUTES **MAKES** 6

Make brekkie muffins following the recipe on page 99, adding 1 tsp ground ginger and 2 tbsp shredded coconut to dry ingredients. Spoon mixture into cases; top with slices of fresh peach and 1 tbsp extra shredded coconut. Bake for 25 minutes or until muffins are cooked when a skewer is inserted and comes out clean. Stand muffins in pan for 5 minutes before transferring to a wire rack to cool.

TIP You will need 1 medium peach (150g) for this recipe.

ORANGE, POPPY SEED & BLUEBERRY MUFFINS

PREP + COOK TIME 40 MINUTES **MAKES** 6

Make brekkie muffins following the recipe on page 99, adding 2 tbsp finely grated orange rind, 1 tbsp poppy seeds and 100g (3oz) blueberries to dry ingredients and replacing the coconut oil with 60g (2oz) melted butter. Spoon mixture into cases. Bake for 30 minutes or until muffins are cooked when a skewer is inserted and comes out clean. Stand muffins in pan for 5 minutes before transferring to a wire rack to cool.

LEMON CURD & WHITE CHOCOLATE MUFFINS

PREP + COOK TIME 45 MINUTES **MAKES** 6

Make brekkie muffins following the recipe on page 99, adding 1 tsp vanilla extract (omit the cinnamon) and 50g (1½oz) chopped white chocolate to dry ingredients and replacing the coconut oil with 60g (2oz) melted butter. Spoon mixture into cases; place 1 tsp gluten-free lemon curd into the centre of each muffin. Bake for 30 minutes or until muffins are cooked when a skewer is inserted and comes out clean. Stand muffins in pan for 5 minutes before transferring to a wire rack to cool. Serve each topped with extra lemon curd.

HAZELNUT, RASPBERRY CHOCOLATE MUFFINS

PREP + COOK TIME 45 MINUTES **MAKES** 6

Make brekkie muffins following the recipe on page 99, replacing the almond meal with 1 cup (100g) hazelnut meal, the coconut oil with 60g (2oz) melted butter, adding 100g (3oz) raspberries with the dry ingredients. Spoon mixture into cases, top with 50g (1½oz) chopped dark chocolate, 3 raspberries each and ¼ cup chopped skinless hazelnuts. Bake for 30 minutes or until muffins are cooked when a skewer is inserted and comes out clean. Stand muffins in pan for 5 minutes before transferring to a wire rack to cool.

You can... MIX UP A DIFFERENT FLAVOURED BATCH OF SCONES BY SIMPLY VARYING THE TYPE OF BERRIES THAT YOU USE. TRY QUARTERED CHERRIES, BLUEBERRIES OR BLACKBERRIES AND SERVE WITH A MATCHING JAM.

Raspberry & choc chunk SCONES

EGG FREE

2 cups (270g) gluten-free self-raising flour
¼ cup (25g) milk powder
80g (2½oz) butter, chopped
1 cup (250ml) buttermilk
100g (3½oz) raspberries
180g (5½oz) good-quality white chocolate, chopped
2 tablespoons gluten-free self-raising flour, extra
2 tablespoons buttermilk, extra
raspberry jam and whipped cream, to serve

1 Preheat oven to 200°C/400°F. Line an oven tray with baking paper.

2 Combine sifted flour and milk powder in a large bowl. Add butter; using your fingertips, rub into flour mixture until it resembles fine breadcrumbs. Make a well in the centre and gently mix in buttermilk until almost combined. Add raspberries and chocolate; stir until just combined.

3 Dust work suface with extra flour. Turn dough out, lightly knead to bring together. Roll out until 1.5cm (¾in) thick. Cut dough out using a 6cm (2½in) gluten-free floured cutter, re-rolling scraps as you go. Place scones, side-by-side, almost touching on tray. Brush with extra buttercream.

4 Bake scones for 12 minutes or until browned lightly and cooked through. Serve immediately with jam and cream.

TIPS Depending on the brand of flour you use, you may need to add extra flour. The scone dough should feel soft and slightly sticky to the touch.

KEEPING Scones are best eaten warm on the day they are made.

PREP + COOK TIME 30 MINUTES **MAKES** 15

DAIRY FREE

Good for... A QUICK AND FILLING BREAKFAST WITH A DAIRY-FREE SPREAD, OR PACKED INTO LUNCH BOXES AS A HEALTHY TREAT.

Carrot, date & pecan MUFFINS

1 Preheat oven to 180°C/350°F. Line a 12-hole (⅓-cup/80ml) muffin pan with paper cases.

2 Reserve 12 pecans; coarsely chop remaining pecans. Combine oil and eggs in a large jug.

3 Sift flour, mixed spice and baking powder into a large bowl. Stir in sugar, almond meal, apricots, dates, carrot, coconut and chopped pecans until well combined. Make a well in the centre, add oil mixture; stir until just combined. Spoon mixture into paper cases; top with reserved pecans.

4 Bake muffins for 30 minutes or until a skewer inserted in the centre comes out clean. Transfer to a wire rack to cool. Drizzle muffins with honey.

KEEPING Muffins are best eaten warm. You can reheat them in the microwave on HIGH (100%) in 5 second bursts until warm.

PREP + COOK TIME 50 MINUTES **MAKES** 12

1 cup (120g) pecan halves
½ cup (125ml) extra virgin olive oil
3 eggs
½ cup (65g) ivory or brown teff flour
1 teaspoon mixed spice
1 teaspoon gluten-free baking powder
½ cup (110g) raw caster (superfine) sugar
½ cup (60g) almond meal
½ cup (75g) dried apricots, chopped coarsely
1 cup (140g) chopped pitted fresh dates
1 medium carrot (120g), grated
⅓ cup (25g) shredded coconut
2 tablespoons honey

Choose... OUR SCONE RECIPE ON THIS PAGE, OR ANY ONE OF THE FOUR SCONE FLAVOUR VARIATIONS ON PAGE 109. WHICHEVER RECIPE YOU CHOOSE, THE SECRET TO GOOD SCONES IS TO NOT OVERWORK THE DOUGH AND TO BAKE IT ONLY UNTIL IT'S BARELY DONE, SO YOU GET A CRISP EXTERIOR AND A FLUFFY INTERIOR.

Corn flake & honey SCONES

1 Preheat oven to 220°C/425°F fan-forced (this recipe must be baked in a fan-forced oven). Line a large oven tray with baking paper.

2 Sift flour, baking powder, xanthan gum and salt into a large bowl. Coarsely grate butter into the bowl. Rub in butter until mixture resembles coarse breadcrumbs. Stir in 1 cup (40g) corn flakes and the macadamias. Stir buttermilk, honey and vanilla together in a small jug. Using a butter knife, cut liquid through flour mixture until it starts to clump. Turn out onto a gluten-free floured surface; knead gently for 30 seconds or until dough just comes together. (Don't over work the dough or it will be tough.)

3 Press dough out until 3cm (1¼in) thick. Using a 6.5cm (2¾in) gluten-free floured cutter, stamp out rounds, pressing dough together as needed to cut out 10 rounds. Scatter with remaining corn flakes.

4 Bake scones for 25 minutes or until top is golden and base sounds hollow when tapped, covering with foil during the last 10 minutes of the cooking time. Serve warm drizzled with extra honey and cream.

KEEPING Scones are best eaten on the day the are made or can be frozen for up to 2 months.

PREP + COOK TIME 40 MINUTES **MAKES** 10

2 cups (540g) gluten-free self-raising flour
1 teaspoon gluten-free baking powder
1 teaspoon xanthan gum
1 teaspoon fine salt
200g (6½oz) very cold butter
1½ cups (60g) corn flakes
½ cup (70g) finely chopped lightly roasted macadmias
2½ cups (625ml) buttermilk
2 tablespoons honey
2 teaspoons vanilla bean paste
extra honey and thick (double) cream, to serve

Healthy SCONE VARIATIONS

SUPER SEEDS

PREP + COOK TIME 40 MINUTES **MAKES** 10

Follow the recipe for scones on page 106, omitting the corn flakes and macadamias; instead stir in 1 tbsp each linseeds (flaxseeds), sunflower seeds, chia seeds and pepitas (pumpkin seed kernels) into sifted flour mixture in step 2. Omit the corn flakes in step 3; instead, sprinkle with 2 tsp each linseeds (flaxseeds), sunflower seeds, chia seeds and pepitas (pumpkin seed kernels). Continue recipe as directed.

LEMON & SULTANA

PREP + COOK TIME 40 MINUTES **MAKES** 10

Follow the recipe for scones on page 106, omitting the corn flakes and macadamias; instead add ⅓ cup sultanas and 1 teaspoon finely grated lemon rind. Omit the corn flakes in step 3; instead, sprinkle with 1 tbsp natural flaked almonds. Continue recipe as directed.

APPLE MAPLE

PREP + COOK TIME 40 MINUTES **MAKES** 10

Follow the recipe for scones on page 106, omitting the corn flakes and macadamias; instead stir in 1 coarsely grated small pink-skinned apple in step 2. Omit the honey; instead add 1 tbsp maple syrup with the buttermilk. Omit the corn flakes in step 3; instead, sprinkle with ¼ cup coarsely chopped pecans. Continue recipe as directed.

CRAISIN & CACAO

PREP + COOK TIME 40 MINUTES **MAKES** 10

Follow the recipe for scones on page 106, omitting the corn flakes and macadamias, and adding 2 tbsp cacao powder with the other dry ingredients when sifting in step 2. After rubbing in the butter, omit the corn flakes and macadamias; instead stir in ½ cup craisins and 2 tbsp cacao nibs. Omit the corn flakes in step 3. Continue recipe as directed. Serve dusted with gluten-free icing sugar.

NUT FREE

You can... REPLACE THE DRIED FIGS WITH OTHER DRIED FRUIT. TRY SULTANAS AND TOP WITH A CLUSTER OF SMALL FRESH GRAPES, OR APRICOTS AND THEIR FRESH COUNTERPART, OR DATES, TOPPED WITH FRESH SLICED BANANA.

Quinoa, fig & maple MUFFINS

½ cup (100g) white quinoa
2 eggs
¾ cup (180ml) pure maple syrup
½ cup (140g) greek yoghurt
2 tablespoons canola oil
1 teaspoon vanilla extract
1 cup (135g) gluten-free self-raising flour
1 teaspoon gluten-free baking powder
1¼ teaspoons ground cinnamon
1 cup (80g) quinoa flakes
¾ cup (140g) coarsely chopped dried figs
3 fresh figs, halved

1 Preheat oven to 180°C/350°F. Lightly grease a 6-hole texas (¾-cup/180ml) muffin pan; line with paper cases.

2 Rinse and drain quinoa. Place quinoa and 1 cup (250ml) water in a small saucepan; bring to the boil over high heat. Reduce heat to low; cook, covered, for 15 minutes or until tender and water is absorbed. Remove from heat; stand for 10 minutes, then fluff with a fork. Cool.

3 Combine eggs, ½ cup (125ml) of the maple syrup, yoghurt, oil and vanilla. Sift flour, baking powder and 1 teaspoon of the cinnamon into a large bowl. Stir in quinoa flakes and chopped figs. Make a well in the centre; stir in the egg mixture and quinoa until just combined. Spoon mixture into paper cases; top with halved figs and sprinkle with remaining ¼ teaspoon cinnamon.

4 Bake muffins for 25 minutes or until a skewer inserted into the centre comes out clean. Serve drizzled with remaining maple syrup.

KEEPING Muffins are best eaten on the day they are made.

PREP + COOK TIME 1 HOUR (+ COOLING) **MAKES** 6

200
APPROX
160
120

Good for... AN EASY-BREEZY BRUNCH MENU, SERVE ALONG WITH POACHED EGGS AND BASIC GLUTEN-FREE BREAD (PAGE 16). FOR A DECADENT DESSERT, TOP WITH DAIRY-FREE CHOCOLATE ICE-CREAM AND SHAVED DARK CHOCOLATE.

DAIRY FREE

Berry & fig SKILLET MUFFIN

40g (1½oz) dairy-free spread
1 teaspoon vanilla bean paste
1 cup (230g) fresh dates, pitted
1 tablespoon ground cinnamon
2 teaspoons finely grated ginger
1 cup (120g) almond meal
400ml can coconut cream
1½ teaspoons gluten-free baking powder
⅓ cup (45g) gluten-free self-raising flour
8 eggs
¼ cup (90g) honey
450g (4½oz) mixed fresh berries (see tip)
1½ cups (420g) coconut yoghurt
2 medium fresh figs (120g), halved

1 Preheat oven to 200°C/400°F. Grease a 1.5 litre (6-cup) skillet or ovenproof dish with a little of the dairy-free spread.

2 Process vanilla, ½ cup (125ml) water, dates, cinnamon, ginger, almond meal, coconut cream, baking powder and flour until smooth.

3 Whisk eggs in a large bowl until light and frothy. Add cinnamon mixture to egg; stir gently to combine. Pour into skillet.

4 Bake muffin for 25 minutes or until risen and firm. Remove and cool for 15 minutes.

5 Meanwhile, heat remaining spread and honey in a large frying pan over medium heat; cook half the berries for 2 minutes or until they release some of their juices.

6 Spoon coconut yoghurt over muffin. Stir figs into berry mixture; spoon fruit mixture over muffin and top with remaining berries. Serve immediately.

TIP We used a mixture of raspberries, blueberries and cherries.

KEEPING Skillet muffin is best made close to serving.

PREP + COOK TIME 40 MINUTES **SERVES** 6

BISCUITS & SLICES

You need... TO USE A GOOD-QUALITY PEANUT BUTTER WITHOUT ADDED SUGAR OR SALT TO GET THE BEST RESULTS. FOR AN EVEN MORE INTENSE PEANUT TASTE, USE A DARK-ROAST NATURAL CRUNCHY PEANUT BUTTER.

Peanut butter COOKIES

1 Preheat oven to 180°C/350°F. Line two oven trays with baking paper.

2 Using a fork, mix peanut butter, sugar, egg, baking powder and vanilla in a medium bowl until well combined.

3 Shape level tablespoons of mixture into balls; place on trays 3cm (1¼in) apart. Flatten slightly with a fork; sprinkle with lightly crumbled salt.

4 Bake cookies for 10 minutes or until golden. Cool on trays.

KEEPING Cookies will keep in an airtight container for up to 1 week.

PREP + COOK TIME 20 MINUTES (+ COOLING) **MAKES** 21

1 cup (280g) crunchy natural peanut butter
⅔ cup (150g) firmly packed brown sugar
1 egg, beaten lightly
1 teaspoon gluten-free baking powder
1 teaspoon vanilla extract
½ teaspoon sea salt flakes

NUT FREE

You need... A 12-HOLE (1½ TABLESPOONS) MADELEINE TIN TO MAKE THIS RECIPE, AVAILABLE FROM GOOD KITCHENWARE SHOPS AND ONLINE.

Gluten-free MADELEINES

125g (4oz) butter, plus 30g (1oz) butter, softened, extra
1 teaspoon gluten-free plain (all-purpose) flour
2 eggs
½ cup (110g) caster (superfine) sugar
1 teaspoon vanilla extract
1 cup (135g) gluten-free plain (all-purpose) flour, extra
¼ teaspoon gluten-free baking powder

GLACÉ ICING
1 cup (160g) gluten-free icing (confectioners') sugar
1 teaspoon soft butter
1 tablespoon lemon juice

1 Preheat oven to 200°C/400°F. Heat butter in a small saucepan until starting to turn golden nut brown. Remove from heat; cool.
2 Combine the extra butter and flour in a bowl. Brush two 12-hole (1½-tablespoon) madeleine pans with the butter and flour mixture. Refrigerate for 5 minutes or until set.
3 Beat eggs, sugar and vanilla in a small bowl with an electric mixer for 5 minutes or until thick and creamy.
4 Meanwhile, sift extra flour and baking powder twice onto a piece of baking paper. Sift flour mixture over the egg mixture; fold into egg mixture with browned melted butter, until just combined. Drop tablespoons of mixture into pan holes.
5 Bake madeleines for 8 minutes or until golden and firm to the touch. Leave in pans for 30 seconds. Invert tray onto a work surface, tap the back of a tray with a wooden spoon to assist in releasing the madeleines from the holes. Transfer madeleines to a wire rack to cool.
6 Meanwhile make glacé icing.
7 Dip one end of each madeleine into icing; place on a baking-paper-covered wire rack; stand for 5 minutes or until set.

glacé icing Sift icing sugar into a small heatproof bowl; stir in butter and enough lemon juice to make a thick paste. Place the bowl over a small saucepan of simmering water; stir until icing is of pouring consistency (do not overheat).

KEEPING Madeleines are best eaten on the day othey are made or uniced madeleines can be frozen for up to 1 month.

PREP + COOK TIME 30 MINUTES **MAKES** 24

You can... OMIT THE PEANUTS OR SWAP THEM FOR COARSELY CHOPPED MACADAMIAS OR ROASTED PEELED HAZELNUT HALVES, IF PREFERRED.

Chocolate peanut caramel SLICE

⅔ cup (90g) gluten-free plain (all-purpose) flour
2 tablespoons cocoa powder
⅓ cup (75g) firmly packed brown sugar
⅓ cup (25g) desiccated coconut
85g (3oz) butter, melted
395g (12½oz) can sweetened condensed milk
2 tablespoons golden syrup
40g (1½oz) butter, extra
¾ cup (105g) roasted salted peanuts
150g (4½oz) dark (semi-sweet) chocolate, chopped coarsely

1 Preheat oven to 180°C/350°F. Grease a 19cm (8in) square cake pan; line base and sides with baking paper, extending the paper 5cm (2in) above sides.
2 Combine sifted flour and cocoa, sugar, and coconut in a medium bowl; stir in melted butter until combined. Spoon into pan; use the back of a spoon to press mixture evenly over base of pan.
3 Bake base for 15 minutes or until golden. Cool.
4 Place condensed milk, syrup and half of the extra butter in a medium saucepan; cook over medium heat, stirring continuously, for 10 minutes or until caramel is thickened and a golden colour. Working quickly, pour caramel over the base in pan; smooth the surface level with a spatula. Press peanuts into caramel with a spatula. Bake for 10 minutes; cool.
5 Place chocolate and remaining extra butter in a medium heatproof bowl over a medium saucepan of simmering water (don't let water touch base of bowl); stir until chocolate melts. Pour chocolate mixture over caramel layer. Cool slice completely before removing from pan and cutting into pieces.

KEEPING Slice will keep refrigerated for up to 1 week.

PREP + COOK TIME 40 MINUTES (+ COOLING) **MAKES** 16

Carrot & almond SLICE

1 Preheat oven to 180°C/350°F. Lightly grease a 20cm x 30cm (8in x 12in) slice pan; line base and long sides with baking paper, extending paper 2cm (¾in) over each side.

2 Process flours, sugar and butter until mixture is crumbly. Add egg and 1 tablespoon iced water; process until ingredients just come together. Lightly knead on a surface dusted with a little gluten-free flour.

3 Roll pastry between two sheets of baking paper until large enough to cover the base and sides of pan. Trim excess pastry and patch any gaps with trimmings if necessary, ensuring that the pastry is even across the base. Prick pastry base all over with a fork. Bake for 20 minutes or until lightly golden and cooked through.

4 Make carrot lemon filling. Spread filling over pastry base.

5 Bake slice for 40 minutes or until golden brown and a skewer inserted into the carrot filling comes out clean. Cool slice in pan on a wire rack for 10 minutes before removing slice to wire rack to cool completely.

6 Make lemon icing. Drizzle slice with icing; stand until icing is set.

carrot lemon filling Beat eggs, sugar, butter and golden syrup in a medium bowl with an electric mixer for 2 minutes or until thick. Stir in combined sifted flour, spices, bicarb and salt. Stir in almond meal and carrot until combined.

lemon icing Sift icing sugar into a small bowl; add enough of the lemon juice to form a thin icing.

PREP + COOK TIME 1 HOUR 30 MINUTES **MAKES** 16

¾ cup (110g) gluten-free plain (all-purpose) flour
⅓ cup (60g) rice flour
1½ tablespoons caster (superfine) sugar
80g (2½oz) cold butter, chopped
1 egg

CARROT LEMON FILLING

2 eggs
⅔ cup (150g) caster (superfine) sugar
160g (5oz) butter, softened
½ cup (175g) golden syrup
1 cup (135g) gluten-free plain (all-purpose) flour
2 teaspoons ground cinnamon
1 teaspoon ground ginger
½ teaspoon ground nutmeg
¼ teaspoon bicarbonate of soda (baking soda)
¼ teaspoon fine sea salt
1½ cups (180g) almond meal
2 medium carrots (240g), grated finely

LEMON ICING

¾ cup (120g) gluten-free icing (confectioners') sugar
1½ tablespoons lemon juice, approximately

NUT FREE

You can... MAKE THESE DELICIOUS BUTTERY COOKIES AS THEY ARE HERE OR TURN TO PAGE 127 FOR IDEAS ON SUBSTITUTE INGREDIENTS TO MAKE FOUR DIFFERENT FLAVOUR VARIATIONS.

Basic COOKIE DOUGH

1 Preheat oven to 180°C/350°F. Line four oven trays with baking paper.

2 Beat butter, brown sugar and vanilla in a medium bowl with an electric mixer until just combined. Add eggs; beat until just combined. Stir in sifted flours, bicarb and xanthan gum, in two batches. Cover; refrigerate for 1 hour.

3 Using wet hands, roll dough into 24 balls. Flatten balls with a fork to 6cm (2½in); place 5cm (2in) apart on trays. Scatter with raw sugar.

4 Bake cookies for 18 minutes or until golden. Cool on trays.

TIP Cookies can be stored in an airtight container for up to 1 week.

PREP + COOK TIME 25 MINUTES (+ REFRIGERATION & COOLING)
MAKES 24

250g (8oz) butter, softened
1 cup (220g) firmly packed brown sugar
2 teaspoons vanilla extract
2 eggs
2½ cups (340g) gluten-free plain (all-purpose) flour
⅓ cup (60g) white rice flour
1 teaspoon bicarbonate of soda (baking soda)
2 teaspoons xanthan gum
2 tablespoons raw caster (superfine) sugar

Butter COOKIE VARIATIONS

LIME COCONUT COOKIES

PREP + COOK TIME 35 MINUTES (+ REFRIGERATION & COOLING) **MAKES** 24

Follow the basic cookie dough on page 124, omitting vanilla extract and replacing with 2 tsp finely grated lime rind. Stir ½ cup (40g) desiccated coconut into the dough. Cover; refrigerate 1 hour. Roll and bake dough according to recipe, omitting raw caster sugar. Cool on tray. Sift ¾ cup (120g) gluten-free icing (confectioners') sugar into a small bowl; stir in 1 tbsp lime juice until smooth, adding more if required to achieve desired consistency. Drizzle icing over cookies; place on a wire rack to set.

WHITE CHOCOLATE & GINGER COOKIES

PREP + COOK TIME 35 MINUTES (+ REFRIGERATION & COOLING) **MAKES** 24

Follow the basic cookie dough on page 124, omitting vanilla extract and replacing with 2 tsp finely grated orange rind. Stir ½ cup white Choc Bits (95g) and ¼ cup (45g) finely chopped glacé ginger into the dough. Cover; refrigerate 1 hour. Roll and bake dough according to recipe, omitting raw caster sugar. Cool on tray. Sift 1 cup (160g) gluten-free icing (confectioners') sugar into a bowl; stir in 1 tbsp orange juice until smooth, adding more if required for desired consistency. Dip top of cookies in icing. Place on a wire rack to set.

CHOC CHIP COOKIES

PREP + COOK TIME 35 MINUTES (+ REFRIGERATION & COOLING) **MAKES** 24

Follow the basic cookie dough on page 124, stirring ¾ cup (140g) dark Choc Bits into the dough. Cover; refrigerate for 1 hour. Roll and bake dough according to recipe, omitting raw caster sugar. Cool on tray. Stir 1 cup (150g) milk Chocolate Melts and 2 tsp vegetable oil in a small heatproof bowl over a saucepan of simmering water (don't let water touch base of bowl) until smooth. Dip cookies in melted chocolate until covered half way up. Place on tray to set.

NUTELLA COOKIES

PREP + COOK TIME 30 MINUTES (+ REFRIGERATION & COOLING) **MAKES** 24

Follow the basic cookie dough on page 124, omitting rice flour and replacing with 2 tbsp chocolate Nutella. Stir ½ cup (95g) milk Choc Bits and ¼ cup (35g) chopped roasted hazelnuts into the dough. Cover; refrigerate 1 hour. Roll and bake according to recipe, omitting raw caster sugar. Cool on tray. Spoon Nutella into a piping bag fitted with a 5mm (¼in) plain nozzle and pipe small mounds onto cookies and finish with a halved hazelnut.

NUT FREE

Good for... LUNCH BOXES AND THOSE WITH NUT ALLERGIES. IF NUTS ARE NOT A CONCERN, YOU CAN SWAP THE TAHINI FOR SMOOTH NATURAL PEANUT BUTTER OR ANY OTHER NUT BUTTER, IF PREFERRED.

Easy chocolate TAHINI SLICE

1 Preheat oven to 180°C/350°F. Grease a 20cm x 30cm (8in x 12in) slice pan; line base and long side with baking paper, extending paper 2cm (¾in) over long sides.

2 Crush Weet-Bix in a large bowl; add desiccated coconut. Sift over buckwheat flour, cocoa and baking powder.

3 Stir sugar, butter, tahini and vanilla in a small saucepan over low heat until sugar dissolves. Add to dry ingredients with egg and mix well. Spoon mixture into prepared pan; press out with your hands to level and smooth surface.

4 Bake slice for 18 minutes or until dry to the touch. Cool completely in pan.

5 Make tahini icing.

6 Spread icing over cooled slice; sprinkle with coconut and sesame seeds; stand for 1 hour or until tahini icing is set. Cut widthways into five, then cut each long slice into four squares.

tahini icing Sift icing sugar and cocoa into a large mixing bowl; stir in tahini and ¼ cup (60ml) boiling water until thick and smooth.

KEEPING Slice will keep in an airtight container for up to 3 days.

PREP + COOK TIME 50 MINUTES (+ COOLING) **MAKES** 20

8 gluten-free Weet-Bix (120g)
1 cup (80g) desiccated coconut
¾ cup (115g) buckwheat flour
2 tablespoons dutch-processed cocoa
1½ teaspoons gluten-free baking powder
¾ cup (165g) raw caster (superfine) sugar
150g (4½oz) butter, chopped
¼ cup (70g) tahini
1 teaspoon vanilla extract
1 egg, beaten lightly
2 tablespoons flaked coconut, toasted
1 tablespoon sesame seeds, toasted

TAHINI ICING
1½ cups (240g) gluten-free icing (confectioners') sugar mixture
2 tablespoons dutch-processed cocoa
1 tablespoon tahini

You can... SUBSTITUTE THE ORANGE BLOSSOM WATER FOR 1 TEASPOON FINELY GRATED ORANGE RIND OR FOR THE SAME AMOUNT OF ROSEWATER. YOU CAN ALSO SCATTER THE BISCUITS WITH ⅓ CUP (45G) ROASTED SLIVERED ALMONDS.

Orange blossom & almond shortbread BISCUITS

2 cups (270g) gluten-free plain (all-purpose) flour
½ cup (90g) rice flour
¾ cup (165g) caster (superfine) sugar
½ teaspoon fine salt
250g (8oz) cold unsalted butter, chopped
1½ tablespoons orange blossom water
200g (6oz) dark chocolate (70% cocoa)

1 Preheat oven to 180°C/350°F. Grease three oven trays; line with baking paper.

2 Process flours, sugar, salt, butter and orange blossom water until ingredients cling together.

3 Place a 2cm (¾in) star-shaped nozzle into a piping bag. In four batches, place the dough inside the bag and pipe 8cm (3¼in) long biscuits onto the trays 3cm (1¼in) apart. (The mixture is quite firm, so you will need to use your thumb to assist with pushing the mixture through the nozzle.) Freeze for 15 minutes.

4 Bake shortbread from frozen for 20 minutes or until lightly browned. Transfer to a wire rack to cool.

5 Meanwhile, place chocolate in a small heatproof bowl over a medium saucepan of simmering water (don't let the water touch base of bowl); stir until smooth and melted. Remove from heat. Dip biscuit ends in the chocolate or alternatively drizzle over the chocolate. Place on a wire rack to set.

KEEPING Biscuits will keep in an airtight container for up to 3 days.

PREP + COOK TIME 50 MINUTES **MAKES** 46

You can... TURN THIS INTO A CAKE BY BAKING THE MERINGUE IN TWO 24CM (9½ IN) SPRINGFORM PANS. SERVE TOPPED WITH FRESH BERRIES.

Chai meringue SLAB

1 cup (160g) gluten-free icing (confectioners') sugar, plus extra to dust
4 chai tea bags
¾ cup (60g) shredded coconut
1 cup (80g) desiccated coconut
1 cup (120g) almond meal
6 egg whites
¾ cup (165g) caster (superfine) sugar

VANILLA BEAN MARSHMALLOW
3 teaspoons powdered gelatine
½ cup (125ml) liquid glucose
¾ cup (165g) caster (superfine) sugar
1 egg white
2 teaspoons vanilla bean paste
2 teaspoons finely grated lime rind

1 Preheat oven to 170°C/340°F. Grease two 20cm x 30cm (8in x 12in) slice pans; line with baking paper.

2 Process icing sugar and chai tea until very fine. Transfer to a bowl; add both types of coconut and almond meal; stir to combine.

3 Whisk egg whites and a pinch of salt in an electric mixer until soft peaks form, then gradually add caster sugar, whisking continuously until thick and glossy. Gently fold in coconut mixture, in two batches.

4 Divide meringue mixture evenly between slice pans; level the surface. Bake for 25 minutes swapping and rotating trays between shelves halfway through cooking time. Lift meringue from pans, using baking paper, and cool on wire racks.

5 Once cool, return one meringue slab, still on baking paper, to a slice pan. Line an oven tray with baking paper. Remove paper from second meringue slab, place top-side up, onto tray.

6 Meanwhile make vanilla bean marshmallow; pour marshmallow over meringue base in the pan and, working quickly, spread marshmallow evenly. Slide second meringue slab from the tray on top. Cover with plastic wrap; stand at room temperature for 4 hours or until set.

7 Lift meringue slab from pan; dust with extra icing sugar. Slide a knife underneath to release meringue from the remaining baking paper then cut into 20 pieces.

vanilla bean marshmallow Place 2 tablespoons water in a heatproof jug, sprinkle in gelatine, then microwave on MEDIUM (50%) in 10-second bursts, mixing well each time until gelatine dissolves completely. Set aside. Place glucose, sugar and ¼ cup (60ml) water in a small saucepan over medium heat. Bring to the boil; boil until mixture reaches 125°C/260°F on a cooking thermometer. Cool slightly. Beat egg white and gelatine mixture in an electric mixer fitted with the whisk attachment on medium speed until frothy. With the motor ruining, in a steady stream, pour in the hot sugar mixture. Continue beating for 8 minutes or until mixture is fluffy and just warm. Swirl vanilla bean paste and lime rind into marshmallow.

DAIRY FREE

KEEPING Chai meringue slab will keep at room temperature in an airtight container for up to 3 days.

PREP + COOK TIME 45 MINUTES **SERVES** 20

You need... AN OVENPROOF FRYING PAN TO MAKE THE BLONDIE. IF YOUR FRYING PAN HAS A PLASTIC OR WOODEN HANDLE, WRAP THE HANDLE IN FOIL TO PROTECT IT BEFORE PUTTING THE PAN INTO THE OVEN.

SKILLET BLONDIE *with honeycomb*

200g (6½oz) good-quality white chocolate, chopped
½ cup (70g) macadamia halves
125g (4oz) butter, chopped
¾ cup (180ml) canned coconut cream
½ cup (110g) caster (superfine) sugar
½ cup (110g) firmly packed brown sugar
1 egg, beaten lightly
1 cup (135g) plain (all-purpose) gluten-free flour
¼ cup (30g) almond meal
½ teaspoon gluten-free baking powder
½ teaspoon bicarbonate of soda (baking soda)
1 cup (80g) desiccated coconut
1½ cups (375ml) thick (double) cream, whisked lightly
pure maple syrup, to serve

HONEYCOMB

1 cup (220g) caster (superfine) sugar
¼ cup (60ml) pure maple syrup
2 teaspoons bicarbonate of soda (baking soda)

1 Preheat oven to 180°C/350°F. Line an oven tray with baking paper.

2 Spread chocolate and macadamias evenly over tray. Roast for 8 minutes or until chocolate caramelises to an even light brown and macadamias are roasted. Cool.

3 Meanwhile, melt butter in a 25cm (10in) wide, 5cm (2in) deep, ovenproof non-stick frying pan over medium heat; cook until the butter starts to turn golden brown. Add coconut cream and sugars; stir until sugars dissolve and mixture is smooth. Cool for 5 minutes. Whisk in egg.

4 Sift flour, almond meal, baking powder and bicarb into a large heatproof bowl. Stir in coconut. Pour in butter mixture; stir until well combined. Stir in caramelised chocolate and roasted macadamias. Pour mixture back into frying pan.

5 Transfer frying pan to oven; bake for 20 minutes or until slightly soft and fudgy in the centre.

6 Meanwhile, make honeycomb.

7 Serve warm blondie topped with cream and honeycomb, drizzled with maple syrup.

honeycomb Line an oven tray with baking paper. Stir sugar, maple syrup and ¼ cup (60ml) water in a medium heavy-based saucepan over low heat until sugar dissolves. Increase heat to medium; boil, without stirring, for 8 minutes or until syrup is a dark golden honey colour (or until it reaches 160°C/325°F on a cooking thermometer). Remove pan from heat; immediately stir in sifted bicarb – the syrup will froth. As soon as the last of the bicarb dissolves, carefully and quickly pour honeycomb onto tray; don't spread the mixture or it will deflate. Cool to room temperature. Break honeycomb into large chunks.

KEEPING Blondie will keep refrigerated for up to 2 days. Warm gently in the oven before serving. Store leftover honeycomb in an airtight container for up to 1 week.

PREP + COOK TIME 50 MINUTES (+ COOLING) **SERVES** 8

DAIRY FREE

EGG FREE

Chocolate & almond COOKIES

1 Preheat oven to 160°C/325°F. Grease two oven trays and line with baking paper.
2 In a large bowl, mix oil, spread and sugar using a fork until combined. Add cocoa and flour; stir until mixture forms a soft dough.
3 Roll 2 tablespoons each of mixture into balls to make 18 balls in total. Place on trays, 3cm (1¼in) apart. Press to flatten slightly, using the palm of your hand. Coat cookies evenly in almonds.
4 Bake for 20 minutes or until firm. Cool cookies on trays for 10 minutes. Transfer to a wire rack; cool completely.

⅓ cup (80ml) almond oil
⅔ cup (190g) almond spread
⅔ cup (150g) firmly packed brown sugar
⅓ cup (35g) cocoa powder
1½ cups (200g) gluten-free plain (all-purpose) flour
1¼ cups (120g) natural flaked almonds, toasted, coarsely chopped

TIPS You can substitute other nut oils or extra virgin olive oil for almond oil. For choc-chip cookies, add 100g (3oz) chopped dark (semi-sweet) chocolate to the mixture.

KEEPING Biscuits will keep in an airtight container for up to 1 week.

PREP + COOK TIME 30 MINUTES **MAKES** 18

You can... SWAP HAZELNUTS AND ORANGE FOR PISTACHIO AND LEMON FOR A FLAVOUR VARIATION. WHEN GRATING CITRUS ENSURE IT IS JUST THE VERY OUTSIDE OF THE RIND, NOT THE WHITE PITH AS THIS IS BITTER.

Pistachio & lemon

SANDWICH COOKIES

1 Preheat oven to 140°C/280°F. Line two large oven trays with baking paper.

2 Process pistachios until finely ground; remove 1 tablespoon of the ground nuts and reserve.

3 Add flours, butter, sugar, milk, salt and rind to processor; pulse until mixture comes together when pressed between fingertips.

4 Transfer dough to a work surface; knead lightly to bring together. Enclose in plastic wrap; refrigerate for 1 hour.

5 Make lemon filling.

6 Roll dough between 2 sheets of baking paper until 4mm (⅙in) thick. Using a 5.5cm (2¼in) cutter, cut dough into 24 rounds, re-rolling dough as necessary until all is used. Transfer rounds to lined trays, 2cm (¾in) apart. Sprinkle half of the cookies with reserved ground pistachios. Refrigerate for 30 minutes.

7 Bake for 20 minutes or until lightly browned. Leave cookies for 5 minutes before transferring to a wire rack to cool.

8 Turn over the cookies without the pistachio top. Pipe 1 teaspoon of lemon filling onto each cookie. Top with remaining cookies.

lemon filling Process ingredients in a small food processor until smooth. Transfer to a piping bag fitted with a 6mm (¼in) fluted nozzle; refrigerate until required.

TIPS If dough becomes too soft while rolling and cutting, refrigerate to firm up. Check the label of the lemon curd to make sure it is egg-free.

KEEPING Cookie dough can be made up to 3 days ahead, stored covered in the fridge or freeze for up to 1 month. Cookies can be made a day ahead, pipe with lemon filling before serving.

PREP + COOK TIME 55 MINUTES (+ REFRIGERATION) **MAKES** 12

½ cup (70g) pistachios
1 cup (135g) gluten-free plain (all-purpose) flour
½ cup (90g) rice flour
125g (4oz) cold butter, chopped
⅓ cup (75g) caster (superfine) sugar
2 tablespoons milk
¼ teaspoon fine sea salt
1 tablespoon finely grated lemon rind

LEMON FILLING

250g (8oz) cream cheese, at room temperature
⅓ cup (100g) lemon curd (see tips)
2 teaspoons lemon juice

EGG FREE

Good for... BREAKFAST ON THE RUN; PACK WITH A YOGHURT FOR A HIGH-FIBRE, SLOW-ENERGY RELEASE MEAL. NIBBLE ON FOR A MORNING SNACK OR KEEP ON HAND TO GET YOU THROUGH THE AFTERNOON SLUMP.

Blueberry & spice
BREAKFAST BARS

EGG FREE

1 Preheat oven to 150°C/300°F. Grease a 20cm x 30cm (8in x 12in) slice pan with baking paper, extending the paper 5cm (2in) over long sides.
2 Discard any blueberry juices from thawing. Pat blueberries dry with paper towel.
3 Place amaranth in a small saucepan with 1½ cups (375ml) water; bring to the boil over medium heat. Reduce heat to low, cook, covered, for 20 minutes or until water is absorbed. Drain through a fine sieve over a bowl; stand for 5 minutes to air-dry. Transfer amaranth to a large bowl while still warm, add blueberries and remaining ingredients. Mix well with a large spoon.
4 Spoon mixture into lined pan; level surface. Bake for 65 minutes or until golden and firm to touch. Remove from the oven, flip mixture over and return to pan. Bake for a further 30 minutes. Leave to cool in pan for 5 minutes before inverting onto a wire rack to cool completely.
5 Using a long sharp knife, cut in half widthways. Cut each half into six 10cm (4in) long bars.

KEEPING Store bars in an airtight container in a cool dry place for up to 3 days. Alternatively freeze; remove 1 hour before eating.

PREP + COOK TIME 2 HOURS 10 MINUTES **MAKES** 12

2 cups (300g) frozen blueberries, thawed
¾ cup (150g) amaranth grain
2½ cups (50g) puffed rice
¾ cup (180ml) honey
¾ cup (110g) sunflower seeds
⅔ cup (130g) pepitas (pumpkin seed kernels)
½ cup (50g) golden flaxseed meal
¼ cup (40g) white chia seeds
50g (1½oz) butter, melted
2 teaspoons mixed spice
2 teaspoons ground ginger
½ teaspoon sea salt flakes

Good for... A MORNING TEA TREAT WITH A CUP OF CHAI TEA OR SERVE IN THE AFTERNOON WITH A STRONG BLACK COFFEE. STORE THE SLICE IN AN AIRTIGHT CONTAINER IN THE FRIDGE FOR UP TO 3 DAYS.

Almond, coconut & PINEAPPLE SLICE

1 Preheat oven to 180°C/350°F. Grease a 20cm x 30cm (8in x 12in) rectangular slice pan; line base and sides with baking paper, extending the paper 5cm (2in) over the sides.

2 Beat butter and sugar in a small bowl with an electric mixer until pale. Add egg, beat until just combined. Stir in combined sifted flours and almonds. Spread mixture into pan. Bake for 30 minutes or until browned and firm. Cool in pan.

3 Meanwhile, coarsely chop pineapple pieces. Spread drained crushed pineapple and chopped pineapple pieces seperately onto two layers of paper towel. Stand for 20 minutes to absorb excess moisture.

4 Spread crushed pineapple over cooled base; top with chopped pieces. Spread yoghurt over pineapple.

5 Bake slice for another 20 minutes or until yoghurt is set. Cool in slice pan. Cut into 16 squares. Serve dusted with cinnamon.

TIPS The pineapple needs to feel dry to touch. Pineapple can be swapped for pie apple or pears, if you like.

PREP + COOK TIME 1 HOUR 10 MINUTES **MAKES** 16 PIECES

125g (4oz) butter, softened
1 cup (220g) caster (superfine) sugar
1 egg, beaten lightly
1 cup (140g) coconut flour
½ cup (65g) gluten-free self-raising flour
2 tablespoons slivered almonds
225g (7oz) can pineapple pieces, drained
440g (14oz) can crushed pineapple, drained
300g (9½oz) greek yoghurt
2 tablespoons ground cinnamon

Very lemony BARS

½ cup (40g) desiccated coconut
150g (4½oz) unsalted butter, melted, cooled
¼ cup (55g) caster (superfine) sugar
1⅔ cups (200g) almond meal
1 egg yolk
1 teaspoon vanilla bean paste
2 tablespoons gluten-free icing (confectioners') sugar
¾ cup (60g) shredded coconut
2 egg whites, beaten lightly

LEMON FILLING

4 eggs
1 cup (220g) caster (superfine) sugar
½ cup (120g) sweetened condensed milk
1 tablespoon finely grated lemon rind (see tip)
½ cup (125ml) lemon juice
1 tablespoon 100% corn (maize) cornflour (cornstarch)
1 tablespoon rice flour
1 teaspoon arrowroot flour

1 Preheat oven to 140°C/280°F. Grease a 20cm x 30cm (8in x 12in) slice pan; line base and long sides with baking paper, extending the paper 2cm (¾in) over sides.

2 Place coconut in lined pan; bake, stirring halfway, for 3 minutes or until golden and toasted. Transfer to a bowl (reserve pan); add butter, sugar, almond meal, egg yolk and vanilla. Stir until mixture forms a dough. Press dough evenly into lined pan using fingertips, then level with the back of a spoon. Bake for 20 minutes or until golden.

3 Meanwhile, make lemon filling.

4 Pour lemon filling over warm base. Bake for a further 30 minutes or until edges start to turn golden brown and filling has set with a slight wobble to it.

5 Meanwhile, combine icing sugar, shredded coconut and egg whites on a small baking-paper-lined oven tray. Bake coconut mixture alongside bars, stirring once, for 15 minutes or until golden brown. Cool.

6 Cool slice in pan for 30 minutes. Transfer to the fridge and chill for at least 2 hours or overnight to set. (Keep coconut crunch separate in an airtight container at room temperature.) Using paper, lift slice from pan. Using a sharp knife, trim edges then cut into 4cm x 10cm (1½in x 4in) pieces to make 14 bars in total. Scatter lemon bars with coconut crunch to serve.

lemon filling Whisk ingredients together in a bowl.

TIP You will need 3 lemons for this recipe.

KEEPING Bars will keep refrigerated in an airtight container for up to 1 week.

PREP + COOK TIME 1 HOUR **MAKES** 14 BARS

Good for... BREAKFAST ON THE RUN. PACK FOR LUNCH AND EAT ALONGSIDE A SIMPLE SALAD WITH CHILLI SAUCE. OR FOR A SUBSTANTIAL DINNER, UP THE VEGIES EVEN FURTHER AND TOP WITH SAUTEED MUSHROOMS AND PESTO.

Five-a-day veg & QUINOA SLICE

NUT FREE

1 Preheat oven to 180°C/350°F. Grease a 20cm (8in) square cake pan; line base and sides with baking paper, extending the paper 5cm (2in) over the sides.

2 Rinse quinoa in a sieve under cold running water. Place quinoa and 1½ cups (375ml) water in a medium saucepan; bring to the boil. Reduce heat to low; cook, covered, for 15 minutes or until quinoa is tender. Drain; cool slightly.

3 Meanwhile, heat olive oil in a medium non-stick frying pan over medium heat; cook bacon and onion, stirring, for 5 minutes or until onion is soft. Add zucchini and carrot; cook stirring for 3 minutes or until softened.

4 Place quinoa and vegetable mixture in a large bowl, add remaining ingredients except tomatoes; stir until combined. Pour mixture into pan; smooth the surface. Press tomatoes into the top.

5 Bake slice for 40 minutes or until browned and firm to touch. Cool in pan. Cut slice into slices to serve.

KEEPING Slice will keep in an airtight container in the fridge for up to 3 days.

PREP + COOK TIME 1 HOUR (+ COOLING) **SERVES** 4

1½ cups (300g) quinoa
2 teaspoons olive oil
3 rindless gluten-free bacon slices (195g), chopped coarsely
1 medium onion (150g), chopped finely
1 medium zucchini (120g), grated coarsely
1 medium carrot (120g), grated coarsely
1 cup (10g) baby spinach
5 eggs, beaten lightly
1 cup (120g) coarsely grated cheddar
1½ tablespoons dijon mustard
250g (8oz) cherry truss tomatoes

CAKES & CUPCAKES

Banana brittle UPSIDE-DOWN CAKE

- 2 cups (440g) caster (superfine) sugar
- ⅓ cup (95g) smooth peanut butter
- 7 small bananas (910g), whole, peeled
- 125g (4oz) sour cream
- ¾ cup (180ml) vegetable oil
- 3 eggs
- ½ cup (80g) ivory teff flour
- ½ cup (70g) gluten-free self-raising flour
- ½ cup (90g) rice flour
- ½ cup (60g) almond meal
- 1 teaspoon bicarbonate of soda (baking soda)
- 2 tablespoons honey
- ½ teaspoon sea salt

1 Preheat oven to 160°C/325°F. Grease a deep, 22cm (8¾in) round cake pan; line base and side with two layers of baking paper.

2 Place ½ cup of the sugar and ¼ cup (60ml) water in a small saucepan. Cook over medium heat, without stirring for 8 minutes or until a caramel colour. Remove from heat, add 1 tablespoon of the peanut butter and stir until smooth. Working quickly, pour peanut caramel over base of lined pan; swirl to coat base evenly.

3 Halve four of the bananas lengthways; arrange over caramel, cut-side down, working from the outside inwards, following the shape of the pan and trimming bananas if necessary.

4 Mash remaining 3 bananas with a fork or potato masher in a large bowl until smooth. Whisk in remaining 1½ cups sugar and ¼ cup peanut butter, followed by sour cream, oil and eggs.

5 Sift over flours, almond meal and bicarb, then fold through the banana mixture until just combined. Pour batter over bananas in cake pan, level the surface.

6 Bake cake for 1 hour 40 minutes or until a skewer inserted into the centre comes out clean. Leave in pan for 5 minutes before inverting onto a wire rack to cool. Serve drizzled with honey and sprinkled with salt.

KEEPING Cake is best eaten on the day it is baked.

PREP + COOK TIME 2 HOURS **SERVES** 14

You can... ALSO BAKE THIS CAKE IN TWO 22CM (9IN) SPRINGFROM PANS OR EIGHT 10CM (4IN) INDIVIDUAL SPRINGFORM PANS, SHORTENING THE COOKING TIME. FOR INDIVIDUAL CAKES SPREAD TOP ONLY OF EACH CAKE WITH FROSTING.

Chocolate, walnut & buckwheat SANDWICH CAKE

1 Preheat oven to 180°C/350°F. Grease two 20cm (8in) round sandwich pans; line bases and sides with baking paper. Line a small oven tray with baking paper.

2 Process flours, baking powder and 1¼ cups (125g) of the walnuts until walnuts are finely ground.

3 Beat butter, sugar and vanilla in a large bowl with an electric mixer until light and creamy. Beat in egg yolks. Fold in ground walnut mixture and chocolate.

4 Beat egg whites in a medium bowl with an electric mixer until soft peaks form; gently fold into chocolate mixture. Spread mixture evenly into pans.

5 Bake for 25 minutes or until cakes spring back when gently pressed in the centre. Leave cakes in pans for 5 minutes, before turning, top-side up, onto wire racks to cool. Meanwhile, place remaining ¼ cup (25g) walnuts on lined tray, drizzle with honey; bake for 5 minutes. Cool and coarsely chop.

6 Make mascarpone cream.

7 Place one cake onto a plate; spread with half the mascarpone cream. Repeat layering with remaining cake and cream. Top with chopped walnuts, drizzle with extra honey.

mascarpone cream Beat cream, sifted icing sugar and rind with an electric mixer until soft peaks form. Fold mascarpone into cream mixture.

KEEPING Cake is best eaten on day it is made.

PREP + COOK TIME 55 MINUTES (+ COOLING) **SERVES** 10

¾ cup (110g) buckwheat flour
⅔ cup (90g) gluten-free self-raising flour
2 teaspoons gluten-free baking powder
1½ cups (150g) walnuts
200g (6½oz) butter, at room temperature, chopped
¾ cup (165g) caster (superfine) sugar
1 teaspoon vanilla extract
6 eggs, separated
150g (4½oz) dark (semi-sweet) chocolate, grated
¼ cup (90g) honey, plus extra to serve

MASCARPONE CREAM
300ml thickened (heavy) cream
⅓ cup (55g) gluten-free icing (confectioners') sugar
2 teaspoons finely grated orange rind
⅔ cup (170g) mascarpone

Berry LAMINGTONS

1 Make blueberry jam.

2 Meanwhile, preheat oven to 180°C/350°F. Grease a 20cm x 30cm (8in x 12in) slice pan; line base and long sides with baking paper, extending the paper 2cm (¾in) over the sides.

3 Beat eggs and caster sugar in a large bowl with an electric mixer for 8 minutes or until mixture is thick and creamy.

4 Triple-sift combined flours. Whisk flour mixture into egg mixture until just combined. Pour mixture into pan.

5 Bake cake for 25 minutes or until cake is dry to the touch and edges are coming away from the sides of the pan. Stand cake in pan for 5 minutes before turning, top-side up, onto a wire rack to cool.

6 Whisk cream and icing sugar in a bowl with an electric mixer until firm peaks form. Cover; refrigerate until required.

7 Trim sponge then cut into 24 x 5cm (2in) squares using a serrated knife. Cut each square in half horizontally. Sandwich squares with 1 teaspoon each blueberry jam, then 2 teaspoons cream, spreading each evenly. Place half the coconut in a shallow bowl. Using a wide pastry brush, carefully brush remaining jam lightly onto a filled sponge square until completely covered. Place sponge into coconut, sprinkling coconut all over to evenly coat square. Repeat with remaining sponge squares, jam and coconut. Using a sharp knife, cut lamingtons in half; serve.

blueberry jam Place blueberries, sugar, rind and ¾ cup (180ml) water in a medium heavy-based saucepan; stir over medium heat, without boiling, until sugar dissolves. Bring to the boil; boil, without stirring, for 10 minutes (scrape the base of the pan occasionally to make sure jam is not sticking). Remove from heat; cool. Transfer jam to a tall jug; blend with a hand-held blender until smooth. Cover; stand at room temperature until required.

KEEPING Sponge and jam can be made a day ahead. Store sponge in an airtight container and refrigerate jam. Assemble lamingtons up to 2 hours ahead of serving.

PREP + COOK TIME 1 HOUR (+ STANDING) **MAKES** 24

6 eggs
⅔ cup (150g) caster (superfine) sugar
⅓ cup (50g) 100% corn (maize) cornflour (cornstarch)
½ cup (65g) gluten-free self-raising flour
⅓ cup (45g) gluten-free plain (all-purpose) flour
2 cups (500ml) pouring cream
1 tablespoon gluten-free icing (confectioners') sugar
3 cups (300g) desiccated coconut

BLUEBERRY JAM
375g (12oz) blueberries
1 cup (220g) jam setting sugar
2 teaspoons finely grated lemon rind

NUT FREE

FOR A DAIRY-FREE OPTION
SWAP POURING CREAM FOR THICK
GLUTEN-FREE COCONUT YOGHURT.

Ricotta, polenta & blueberry CAKE

1 Preheat oven to 180°C/350°F. Grease a 20cm x 30cm (8in x 12in) slice pan; line base and sides with baking paper.

2 Reserve 2 tablespoons of the sugar for topping. Combine remaining sugar, almond meal, polenta and baking powder in a large bowl.

3 Whisk ricotta, eggs, oil, rind and vanilla until smooth. Stir into dry ingredients until just combined. Spoon mixture into pan. Scatter with blueberries then sprinkle with reserved sugar.

4 Bake for 1 hour or until a skewer inserted into the centre comes out clean. Leave cake in pan for 10 minutes before transferring, top-side up, onto a wire rack to cool.

5 Make whipped ricotta.

6 Serve cake cut into squares, topped with whipped ricotta.

whipped ricotta Process ingredients until smooth and creamy.

KEEPING Cake is best eaten on day it is baked.

PREP + COOK TIME 1 HOUR 10 MINUTES (+ COOLING) **SERVES** 10

¾ cup (165g) raw caster (superfine) sugar
1½ cups (180g) almond meal
⅔ cup (100g) fine polenta
3 teaspoons gluten-free baking powder
1 cup (240g) fresh firm ricotta
2 eggs
½ cup (125ml) lightly-flavoured extra virgin olive oil
2 teaspoons finely grated lemon rind
2 teaspoons vanilla extract
200g (6½oz) blueberries

WHIPPED RICOTTA

1 cup (240g) fresh firm ricotta
2 tablespoons milk
2 tablespoons caster (superfine) sugar
1 teaspoon vanilla extract

Choose... MACAROONS IN PALE SHADES: WHITE, CREAM, DUSTY PINK, COFFEE OR MILK CHOCOLATE TO COMPLEMENT THE CUPCAKES.

Cherry & macadamia CUPCAKES

1 Preheat oven to 180°C/350°F. Line a 12-hole (⅓ cup/80ml) cupcake pan with paper cases. Thaw frozen cherries in a small bowl; reserve juices. Chop cherries coarsely.

2 Sift flour, sugar, bicarb, xanthan gum and salt into a medium bowl. In a separate bowl, whisk sour cream, eggs, milk, oil and vanilla. Add dry ingredients; stir to combine. Fold through macadamias and the chopped cherries.

3 Spoon ¼ cup batter into each paper case. Bake for 20 minutes or until a skewer inserted into the centre of a cake comes out clean. Transfer to a wire rack to cool.

4 Meanwhile, make buttercream.

5 To decorate, pipe buttercream over cupcakes and level slightly. Top each with a macaroon and drizzle with maple syrup.

buttercream Beat butter with an electric mixer until pale. Add brown sugar and vanilla and beat until pale and very fluffy. Transfer to a piping bag fitted with a 1.5cm (¾in) plain nozzle.

PREP + COOK TIME 35 MINUTES **MAKES** 12

½ cup (90g) frozen pitted cherries
1⅓ cups (180g) gluten-free self-raising flour
⅔ cup (150g) caster (superfine) sugar
½ teaspoon bicarbonate of soda (baking soda)
½ teaspoon xanthan gum
½ teaspoon fine sea salt
½ cup (120g) sour cream
2 eggs
¼ cup (60ml) milk
¼ cup (60ml) vegetable oil
2 teaspoons vanilla bean paste
12 gluten-free macaroons (90g)
⅓ cup (45g) unsalted macadamias, roasted, crushed
2 tablespoons maple syrup

BUTTERCREAM

150g (4½oz) butter, softened
¾ cup (165g) firmly packed brown sugar
½ teaspoon vanilla bean paste

Good for... DESSERT WITH GREEK OR FROZEN YOGHURT. MIX UP THE FLAVOURS BY USING PLUMS AND PEACHES AS SUBSTITUTES FOR NECTARINES, AND HAZELNUT MEAL IN PLACE OF THE ALMOND MEAL.

Nectarine & chilli CAKES

1½ cups (525g) golden syrup
2 fresh long red chillies, sliced thinly on the diagonal
2 teaspoons finely grated lime rind
1½ tablespoons lime juice
3 medium nectarines (510g), halved, stones removed, sliced thinly
225g (7oz) butter, chopped, softened
1 cup (220g) caster (superfine) sugar
4 eggs
1 teaspoon vanilla bean paste
1¼ cups (170g) gluten-free self-raising flour
⅓ cup (40g) almond meal
2 tablespoons milk

1 Preheat oven to 170°C/340°F. Grease a 6-hole texas (¾-cup/180ml) muffin pan; line bases with baking paper.

2 Stir golden syrup, chilli, rind and juice in a medium saucepan over low-medium heat for 3 minutes. Place 2 tablespoons of the syrup mixture in the base of each pan hole; reserve remaining syrup to serve. Cover base of pans with overlapping nectarine slices.

3 Beat butter and sugar in a large bowl with an electric mixer until pale and creamy. Add eggs, one at a time, beating well after each addition. Beat in vanilla. Fold in combined sifted flour and almond meal, then milk until well combined. Spoon mixture into pan holes.

4 Bake cakes for 25 minutes or until a skewer inserted in the centre of a cake comes out clean. Leave cakes in pan for 5 minutes before inverting onto a wire rack to cool.

5 Reheat remaining chilli syrup; drizzle over cakes before serving.

KEEPING Cakes can be made a day ahead; store in an airtight container at room temperature.

PREP + COOK TIME 1 HOUR **MAKES** 6

You can... VARY THE TYPE OF CITRUS USED IN THIS RECIPE SO LONG AS THE WEIGHT REMAINS THE SAME. TRY A TANGELO OF THE SAME WEIGHT FOR A MORE TANGY TASTE OR 3 SMALL MANDARINS INSTEAD OF THE ORANGE.

Orange & white chocolate CAKE

1 large orange (300g)
4 eggs
50g (1½oz) butter, melted
200g (6½oz) white chocolate, grated coarsely
1 cup (220g) caster (superfine) sugar
2 cups (240g) almond meal
1½ teaspoons gluten-free baking powder
100g (3oz) white chocolate, extra, grated coarsely

1 Place washed and unpeeled whole orange in a medium saucepan with enough water to cover. Bring to the boil; simmer for 1½ hours or until orange is tender, topping up pan with boiling water as needed to keep orange covered. Drain; cool orange to room temperature. Discard ends from orange. Halve orange; discard seeds.
2 Preheat oven to 160°C/325°F. Grease a 20cm (8in) round springform cake pan; line base and side with baking paper.
3 Process orange, including rind, until pulpy. Add eggs and butter; process until smooth. Transfer mixture to a large bowl. Stir in white chocolate, sugar, almond meal and sifted baking powder. Pour mixture into pan.
4 Bake cake for 1 hour 20 minutes or until a skewer inserted into the centre comes out clean. Cool cake in pan for 25 minutes.
5 Remove cake from pan and sprinkle with extra grated chocolate. Serve warm or at room temperature.

TIP Depending on the design of the springform pan you're using, lock the base in upside down so that the base is level; this will make it easier to remove the cake from the base.

KEEPING Cake is best eaten on the day it is made.

PREP + COOK TIME 3 HOURS (+ COOLING & STANDING) **SERVES** 12

DAIRY FREE

Good with... A DOLLOP OF SOY YOGHURT FOR AFTERNOON TEA OR SERVE WARM WITH A GENEROUS SCOOP OF DAIRY-FREE VANILLA OR RASPBERRY ICE-CREAM FOR DESSERT. OR PACK INTO AN AIRTIGHT CONTAINER FOR A PORTABLE TREAT!

Jammy hummingbird CAKES

1 cup (135g) gluten-free self-raising flour
1 cup (135g) gluten-free plain (all-purpose) flour
½ teaspoon bicarbonate of soda (baking soda)
½ cup (110g) firmly packed brown sugar
2 teaspoons mixed spice
1 teaspoon ground cinnamon
1 medium ripe banana (200g), mashed
275g (9oz) crushed pineapple in juice
½ cup (125ml) almond milk
⅓ cup (80ml) extra virgin olive oil
3 eggs
1 teaspoon vanilla bean paste
1 cup (100g) walnuts, roasted, chopped coarsely
¾ cup (250g) apricot jam
1 cup (50g) flaked coconut, toasted

1 Preheat oven to 200°C/400°F. Grease six 10cm (4in) round springform cake pans; line base and side with baking paper, extending the paper 1cm (½in) over sides. Place pans on an oven tray.

2 Sift flours, bicarb, sugar and spices into a large bowl. Combine banana, undrained pineapple, almond milk, olive oil, eggs and vanilla in a separate bowl. Add pineapple mixture to dry ingredients; mix to combine (the batter will be very wet). Divide ¾ cup of the mixture evenly between each pan. Divide walnuts among pans; using a skewer, loosely stir nuts through batter.

3 Bake cakes for 30 minutes or until a skewer inserted into the centre of the cakes comes out clean and cakes spring back when pushed. Stand cakes for 40 minutes.

4 Place jam in a small saucepan; cook over medium-high heat without stirring, for 4 minutes or until mixture comes to the boil. Stir with a wooden spoon until smooth. Divide hot jam among cake pans. Scatter cakes with coconut and stand for a further 30 minutes or until jam is set.

5 Release side of cake pans; transfer cakes to plates to serve.

KEEPING Cakes will keep in an aritight container for up to 3 days.

PREP + COOK TIME 55 MINUTES (+ COOLING) **MAKES** 6

Good for... A DECADENT BRUNCH. TOAST SLICES FIRST IN A SANDWICH PRESS BEFORE PILING ON THE TOPPINGS, OR SERVE FRESH SLICES OF CAKE FOR AFTERNOON TEA WITH CUPS OF FRESHLY BREWED EARL GREY TEA.

Almond & strawberry POUND CAKE

200g (6½oz) unsalted butter, softened
1 cup (220g) caster (superfine) sugar
3 eggs
1½ cups (200g) gluten-free self-raising flour
1 teaspoon cream of tartar
1 cup (120g) almond meal
¼ cup (60ml) milk
200g (6½oz) crème fraîche

STRAWBERRY JAM

500g (1lb) strawberries, hulled
1 cup (220g) caster (superfine) sugar
¼ cup (60ml) lemon juice

1 Preheat oven to 170°C/340°F. Grease a 12.5cm x 23cm (5in x 9¼in), 1.5 litre (6-cup) loaf pan; line base and sides with two layers of baking paper, extending the paper 5cm (2in) over sides.

2 Beat butter and sugar in a medium bowl with an electric mixer until light and fluffy. Add eggs one at a time, beating well between each addition. Gently fold in the sifted flour, cream of tartar, almond meal and the milk. Spoon cake mixture into loaf pan, level the surface.

3 Bake cake for 50 minutes or until a skewer inserted in the centre comes out clean. Leave cake in pan for 5 minutes, before turning, top-side up, onto a wire rack to cool.

4 Meanwhile, make strawberry jam.

5 Serve pound cake sliced, topped with crème fraîche and strawberry jam.

strawberry jam Place 400g (12½oz) of the strawberries in a small saucepan with sugar and juice. Bring to the boil. Reduce heat to medium; simmer for 15 minutes or until strawberries are very soft and the syrup has thickened slightly. Stir in remaining strawberries.

PREP + COOK TIME 1 HOUR 15 MINUTES **SERVES** 12

You can... FOR A DAIRY-FREE OPTION, USE 'TOFUTTI BETTER THAN CREAM CHEESE', A TOFU-BASED CREAM CHEESE SUBSTITUTE, AVAILABLE IN THE REFRIGERATED SECTION OF HEALTH FOOD STORES AND SOME SUPERMARKETS.

CARROT CAKE *with frosting*

1 Preheat oven to 180°C/350°F. Grease a deep 22cm (9in) round cake pan; line base and side with baking paper.

2 Sift flour, almond meal, bicarb, cinnamon and nutmeg into a large bowl; stir in sugar, carrot and walnuts. Add combined eggs and oil; stir until smooth. Pour mixture into pan; smooth the surface.

3 Bake cake for 1 hour and 10 minutes or until a skewer inserted in the centre comes out clean. Stand cake in pan 5 minutes; turn, top-side up, onto a wire rack to cool.

4 Make frosting; spread on top of cooled cake. Dust cake with extra nutmeg.

frosting Beat cream cheese and rind in a small bowl with an electric mixer until light and fluffy. Gradually beat in sifted icing sugar until smooth.

KEEPING Cake will keep refrigerated for up to 3 days.

PREP + COOK TIME 1 HOUR 30 MINUTES (+ COOLING) **SERVES** 12

- 2½ cups (335g) gluten-free self-raising flour
- ½ cup (60g) almond meal
- ½ teaspoon bicarbonate of soda (baking soda)
- 2 teaspoons ground cinnamon
- 1 teaspoon finely grated fresh nutmeg, plus extra to dust
- 1⅓ cups (295g) firmly packed brown sugar
- 3 cups (450g) coarsely grated carrot
- 1 cup (120g) coarsely chopped walnuts
- 3 eggs
- 1 cup (250ml) extra virgin olive oil

FROSTING

- 200g (6oz) cream cheese, softened
- 2 teaspoons finely grated lemon rind
- 3 cups (480g) gluten-free icing (confectioners') sugar

VANILLA CUPCAKES *with variations*

1 cup (220g) caster (superfine) sugar
1 teaspoon vanilla extract
3 eggs
125g (4oz) dairy-free spread
1½ cups (200g) gluten-free self-raising flour
½ cup (35g) gluten-free baby rice cereal
¼ cup (60ml) soy milk

VANILLA FROSTING
125g (4oz) dairy-free spread
1 teaspoon vanilla extract
1½ cups (240g) gluten-free icing (confectioners') sugar

1 Preheat oven to 180°C/350°F. Line 14 holes of two 12-hole (⅓-cup/80ml) muffin pans with paper cases.
2 Beat sugar, vanilla and eggs in a bowl with an electric mixer for 5 minutes or until thick and pale. Add dairy-free spread, a little at a time, beating well between additions; mixture may look curdled at this stage. Gradually add sifted flour, rice cereal and soy milk. Spoon mixture evenly into paper cases.
3 Bake cupcakes for 20 minutes. Leave cupcakes in pan for 5 minutes before turning, top-side up, onto a wire rack to cool.
4 Meanwhile, make vanilla frosting.
5 Spread frosting over cooled cupcakes.

vanilla frosting Beat dairy-free spread and vanilla in a bowl with an electric mixer until pale. Beat in sifted icing sugar in two batches, until well combined and smooth.

VARIATIONS

blueberry Stir in ¾ cup frozen blueberries to vanilla cupcake mixture after adding the soy milk. Bake as directed. Serve dusted with gluten-free icing (confectioners') sugar, if you like.

coconut cherry Stir in 1½ tbsp desiccated coconut, 1½ tbsp sifted cocoa powder, 1½ tbsp soy milk and 50g (1½oz) finely chopped dairy-free dark (semi-sweet) chocolate into the vanilla cupcake mixture after adding the baby rice cereal. Spoon into cases. Top with ½ cup (100g) halved glacé cherries, ½ cup (40g) shredded coconut and an extra 50g (1½oz) chopped dark dairy-free chocolate. Bake as directed.

apple cinnamon Quarter and core 1 small red apple, then cut into thin slices. Arrange two or three slices on top of the vanilla cupcake mixture after spooning into paper cases. Combine 2 tsp ground cinnamon and 2 tbsp raw sugar; sprinkle cupcakes with cinnamon mixture. Bake as directed.

PREP + COOK TIME 45 MINUTES (+ COOLING) **MAKES** 12

DAIRY FREE

You can... USE THIS RECIPE AS A BASE FOR AN ORANGE AND BLUEBERRY CAKE; SUBSTITUTE ORANGE FOR LEMON RIND AND BLUEBERRIES FOR RASPBERRIES. FOR THE GLAZE, YOU WILL NEED 4 SMALL PASSIONFRUIT.

RASPBERRY CAKE

with passionfruit glaze

125g (4oz) dairy-free spread
¾ cup (165g) caster (superfine) sugar
1 tablespoon finely grated lemon rind
3 eggs
1¾ cups (235g) gluten-free self-raising flour
¼ cup (60ml) soy milk
¾ cup (100g) frozen raspberries

PASSIONFRUIT GLAZE
2 teaspoons (10g) dairy-free spread
1 cup (160g) gluten-free icing (confectioners') sugar
⅓ cup (60ml) passionfruit pulp (see above)

1 Preheat oven to 190°C/375°F. Grease a 21cm (8½in) baba or bundt pan well with dairy-free spread; dust with a little gluten-free flour, shake out excess.
2 Beat dairy-free spread, sugar and rind in a medium bowl with an electric mixer until light and fluffy. Beat in eggs, one at a time, until just combined. Stir in sifted flour and the milk, alternately, in batches. Stir in raspberries. Spread mixture into pan.
3 Bake for 45 minutes or until a skewer inserted into the centre of the cake comes out clean.
4 Stand cake in pan for 5 minutes before turning onto a wire rack over an oven tray. Cool to room temperature.
5 Make passionfruit glaze.
6 Spoon passionfruit glaze over cake allowing some to drip down the sides.

passionfruit glaze Stir ingredients in a small bowl until smooth.

KEEPING Cake is best eaten on the day it is made.

PREP + COOK TIME 1 HOUR 15 MINUTES **SERVES** 8

Vanilla ice-cream

BROWNIE STACK

1 Preheat oven to 180°C/350°F. Grease a 20cm x 30cm (8in x 12in) slice pan; line base and two long sides with baking paper, extending the paper 2cm (¾in) over the sides.
2 Beat egg yolks, ½ cup of the sugar and the vanilla in a small bowl with an electric mixer for 5 minutes or until thick and pale. Fold in chocolate. Beat egg whites in a clean small bowl with electric mixer until soft peaks form. Gradually add remaining sugar, beating after each addition until sugar dissolves and mixture is glossy and firm. Gently fold egg white mixture into egg yolk mixture. Add almond meal, combined sifted baking powder and cocoa, and butter; fold into the chocolate mixture. Pour brownie mixture into pan.
3 Bake brownie for 20 minutes or until a skewer inserted into the centre comes out clean. Leave brownie in pan for 10 minutes before turning, top-side up, onto a wire rack to cool.
4 Line a 10cm x 20cm (4in x 8in) straight-sided loaf pan or terrine mould with plastic wrap. Cut brownie into thirds lengthways. Place one piece of brownie in pan. Spread half the softened ice-cream over. Repeat with another brownie layer and remaining ice-cream. Top with final piece of brownie; cover. Freeze for 2 hours or until firm.
5 Meanwhile, make pomegranate syrup.
6 Top with blackberries and drizzle with pomegranate syrup.

pomegranate syrup Combine ingredients in a medium saucepan over medium heat; bring to the boil. Reduce heat to low; simmer syrup for 25 minutes or until reduced to 1 cup. Cool to room temperature.

KEEPING Brownie can be made a day ahead; store in an airtight container until ready to use.

PREP + COOK TIME 1 HOUR 30 MINUTES (+ COOLING & FREEZING)
SERVES 10

3 eggs, separated
⅔ cup (150g) caster (superfine) sugar
1 teaspoon vanilla extract
200g (6½oz) dark chocolate (70% cocoa), melted, cooled
½ cup (60g) almond meal
½ teaspoon baking powder
2 tablespoons cocoa powder
50g (1½oz) butter, melted
1 litre (4 cups) gluten-free vanilla ice-cream, softened
250g (8oz) blackberries

POMEGRANATE SYRUP
2 cups (500ml) pomegranate juice
⅔ cup (150g) caster (superfine) sugar
2 teaspoons lemon juice

You may... NEED TO PURCHASE TWO BUNCHES OF RHUBARB TO ENSURE THAT ALL THE STALKS ARE OF AN EVEN THICKNESS TO ACHIEVE THE STRIKING PATTERNED TOP. SELECT BUNCHES OF RHUBARB WITH THE REDDEST STEMS.

Rhubarb upside-down CAKE

1 Preheat oven to 180°C/350°F. Grease a deep 23cm (9in) square cake pan; line base and sides with baking paper.

2 Cut rhubarb into 23cm (9in) long pieces (see tips). Combine rhubarb, sugar and melted butter in a large bowl; stand for 5 minutes. Using the picture as a guide, arrange rhubarb in a single layer over base of lined pan; top with any remaining sugar mixture.

3 Beat the softened butter, vanilla and extra sugar in a medium bowl with an electric mixer until pale and fluffy. Beat in eggs, one at a time, until well combined. Stir in sifted flour and custard powder alternately with the buttermilk.

4 Dollop cake mixture gently over top of rhubarb then smooth surface.

5 Bake cake for 55 minutes or until a skewer inserted into centre comes out clean. Leave cake in pan for 15 minutes before carefully inverting onto a serving plate or cutting board. Serve slices of cake warm with ice-cream, if you like.

TIPS If rhubarb stalks are thick, cut in half lengthways before tossing in the sugar and butter. Place cut side up in base of pan.

PREP + COOK TIME 1 HOUR 5 MINUTES **SERVES** 8

400g (12½oz) rhubarb
½ cup (110g) caster (superfine) sugar
40g (1½oz) butter, melted, cooled
185g (6oz) butter, at room temperature
1 teaspoon vanilla extract
1 cup (220g) caster (superfine) sugar, extra
3 eggs
1⅔ cups (225g) gluten-free self-raising flour
⅓ cup (40g) gluten-free custard powder
½ cup (125ml) buttermilk
1 litre (4 cups) vanilla ice-cream, to serve, optional

Good for... DESSERT WITH THICK CREAM OR GLUTEN-FREE VANILLA ICE-CREAM. OR KEEP IT DAIRY-FREE AND MAKE YOUR OWN 'NICE-CREAM' BY PROCESSING OR BLENDING FROZEN RIPE BANANAS UNTIL VERY SMOOTH.

Banana chocolate PECAN CAKE

DAIRY FREE

1 Preheat oven to 180°C/350°F. Grease a 21cm (8½in) bundt pan well with a little dairy-free spread.

2 Beat spread and sugar in a small bowl with an electric mixer until light and fluffy. Add eggs, one at a time; beat until combined. Mixture will split at this stage but will come back together once flour is added.

3 Transfer mixture to large bowl, stir in vanilla and banana; stir until well combined. Stir in the sifted flour, cocoa, bicarb, almond milk, chopped pecans and chocolate, in two batches. Pour mixture into pan; smooth surface.

4 Bake cake for 1 hour or until a skewer inserted in the centre comes out clean. Turn cake onto a wire rack over an oven tray.

5 Meanwhile, stir dulce de leche in a small bowl with 2 tablespoons water until a drizzling consistency.

6 Spoon caramel over top of cake allowing some to drip down the side.

TIPS You will need two small bananas for this recipe. If you're not dairy-free you can replace the dairy-free spread with butter and rice milk with cow's milk.

KEEPING Cake without caramel can be made a day ahead.

PREP + COOK TIME 1 HOUR 15 MINUTES (+ COOLING) **SERVES** 12

185g (6oz) dairy-free spread
1¼ cups (275g) caster (superfine) sugar
3 eggs
1 teaspoon vanilla extract
¾ cup mashed banana (see tips)
2¼ cups (365g) gluten-free self-raising flour
⅓ cup (35g) cocoa powder
¼ teaspoon bicarbonate of soda (baking soda)
½ cup (125ml) almond milk
½ cup (60g) coarsely chopped pecans
90g (3oz) dairy-free dark chocolate, chopped
¾ cup (105g) dulce de leche

You can... SERVE THE CHEESECAKE UNADORNED IF YOU LIKE. OR USE IT AS A VEHICLE FOR WHATEVER FRUIT IS IN SEASON. TRY A MIX OF FIGS AND BLUEBERRIES IN LATE SUMMER OR A MIXTURE OF RED BERRIES AND CHERRIES.

New york CHEESECAKE

1 Process biscuits to fine crumbs; add butter, process until combined. Spoon mixture evenly over base of a greased 20cm (8in) round springform pan; press firmly with a straight-sided glass or bottle. Place pan on an oven tray; refrigerate until required.

2 Preheat oven to 160°C/325°F.

3 Beat eggs and sugar in a small bowl with an electric mixer until thick and creamy. Beat cream cheese and vanilla in a medium bowl with an electric mixer until smooth. Add egg mixture to cream cheese mixture; beat until combined. Pour over base in pan.

4 Bake cheesecake for 40 minutes or until still slightly wobbly in the centre. Turn off oven; cool in oven with the door ajar. Refrigerate for 3 hours or overnight.

5 Serve cheesecake topped with fresh raspberries.

TIP You could swap raspberries for blueberries, if you like.

KEEPING Cheesecake will keep refrigerated for up to 2 days.

PREP + COOK TIME 1 HOUR (+ COOLING & REFRIGERATION)
SERVES 12

155g (5oz) packet gluten-free ginger nut biscuits
50g (1½oz) butter, melted
4 eggs
¾ cup (165g) caster (superfine) sugar
500g (1lb) cream cheese, softened
1 teaspoon vanilla bean paste
500g (1lb) raspberries

NUT FREE

Good for... AFTERNOON TEA WITH HEAPED SPOONFULS OF THICK CREAM OR COCONUT OR GREEK YOGHURT. SERVE WARM AS A DESSERT TOPPED WITH SCOOPS OF COCONUT ICE-CREAM OR DRIZZLED WITH THICK CARAMEL SAUCE.

Upside-down pineapple GINGER BEER LOAF

1 Preheat oven to 160°C/325°F fan-forced (this recipe must be baked in a fan-forced oven). Grease a 13cm x 26cm (5¼in x 10½in) (top measurement) loaf pan.

2 Melt 25g (¾oz) of the butter in a saucepan; pour into lined pan, rotating pan to coat the base of pan. Sprinkle with ¼ cup (55g) of the sugar. Drain pineapple and pat slices dry on paper towel. Arrange pineapple slices slightly overlapping along base.

3 Beat remaining butter and remaining sugar in a medium bowl with an electric mixer until light and creamy. Beat in eggs one at a time. Fold in sifted flour, baking powder, spices and ginger beer. Spread mixture into pan.

4 Bake loaf for 45 minutes. Leave in pan for 10 minutes, before turning onto a wire rack to cool slightly. Serve warm.

KEEPING Loaf is best eaten on the day it is made.

PREP + COOK TIME 1 HOUR **SERVES** 8

- **150g (4½oz) butter, at room temperature**
- **1 cup (220g) firmly packed brown sugar**
- **225g (7oz) can pineapple slices in natural juice**
- **2 eggs**
- **2½ cups (335g) gluten-free self-raising flour**
- **1 teaspoon gluten-free baking powder**
- **¾ teaspoon ground cardamom**
- **1 teaspoon ground ginger**
- **¾ cup (180ml) ginger beer**

You can... COMBINE THE PEANUT BUTTER WITH 1 TABLESPOON PURE MAPLE SYRUP FOR THE FROSTING, IF YOU HAVE A SWEET TOOTH. ALSO YOU CAN USE A NATURAL CRUNCHY PEANUT BUTTER INSTEAD OF SMOOTH, IF YOU PREFER.

CHOCOLATE CAKE

with salted peanut butter frosting

1 Preheat oven to 180°C/350°F. Grease a 20cm (8in) round springform pan; line base with baking paper.

2 Whisk sifted cocoa, ½ cup (125ml) boiling water, salt flakes and vanilla in a jug until combined.

3 Beat coconut sugar, eggs and oil in a small bowl with an electric mixer until creamy. Add almond meal and cocoa mixture; stir until smooth. Pour into pan.

4 Bake cake for 45 minutes or until a skewer inserted into the centre comes out almost clean. Cool cake in pan.

5 Spread peanut butter over top of cake. Serve cake sprinkled with extra salt.

KEEPING Cake will keep in an airtight container for up to 3 days or can be frozen for up to 3 months.

PREP + COOK TIME 1 HOUR (+ COOLING) **SERVES** 10

½ cup (50g) cocoa powder
1 teaspoon sea salt flakes
2 teaspoons vanilla extract
1 cup (160g) coconut sugar
3 eggs
⅔ cup (160ml) olive oil
1½ cups (180g) almond meal
½ cup (140g) smooth natural peanut butter, warmed
sea salt flakes, extra, to serve

DAIRY FREE

Good for... BIRTHDAY PARTIES, WEDDINGS OR OTHER SPECIAL OCCASIONS. SERVE AS A DECADENT DESSERT CAKE WITH SOUR CREAM AND THE CHERRIES AND CHERRY SYRUP SPOONED OVER. THE CAKE WILL FREEZE WELL FOR UP TO 1 MONTH.

CHOCOLATE CAKE

with sour cherry ganache

1 Preheat oven to 180°C/350°F. Grease a 20cm (8in) round cake pan; line base and side with baking paper. Drain cherries, reserving ½ cup (125ml) juice for cake batter, ¾ cup for the ganache and remaining juice and cherries for syrup.

2 Place chocolate and butter in a heatproof bowl over a saucepan of simmering water (do not let the bottom of the bowl touch water); stir until melted and smooth.

3 Beat eggs and sugar with an electric mixer until smooth. Add sour cream, chocolate mixture, almond meal, flour and reserved ½ cup cherry juice. Beat for 30 seconds or until smooth and combined.

4 Pour batter into cake pan. Bake for 40 minutes, cover cake with foil, cook for a further 30 minutes or until a skewer inserted into the centre comes out with soft sticky crumbs and cake is puffed with a few small cracks. Stand cake, covered, to cool completely in the pan.

5 Make chocolate cherry ganache.

6 Combine remaining syrup and cherries in a small saucepan with the extra sugar. Bring to the boil over medium heat, stirring to dissolve sugar. Simmer for 6 minutes or until thickend. Cool.

7 Spread ganache evenly over top of cooled cake allowing some to drip down the side. Serve with reduced syrup and cherries.

chocolate cherry ganache Bring reserved ¾ cup cherry juice and cream almost to the boil in a small saucepan; add chocolate, stir until melted and smooth. Stand until thickened to a coating consistency.

KEEPING Cake will keep refrigerated for up to 5 days.

PREP + COOK TIME 1 HOUR 15 MINUTES **SERVES** 12

670g (1¼lb) pitted morello cherries in syrup
360g (11½oz) dark chocolate (70% cocoa), chopped coarsely
250g (8oz) butter, chopped
3 eggs
1 cup (220g) firmly packed brown sugar
250g (8oz) sour cream
2 cups (240g) almond meal
1 cup (135g) gluten-free self-raising flour
¾ cup (165g) firmly packed brown sugar, extra

CHOCOLATE CHERRY GANACHE
1 cup (250ml) pouring cream
200g (6½oz) dark chocolate (70% cocoa), chopped finely

SPECIAL OCCASIONS

You can... VARY THE PASTRY DECORATIONS ON THE PIES BY CUTTING OUT 6CM (2½ IN) ROUNDS, THEN CUTTING OUT 5.5CM (2¼ IN) STARS FROM WITHIN THE ROUND; USE BOTH STARS AND STAR CUT-OUTS TO DECORATE.

Chocolate fruit mince PIES

You will need to make chocolate fruit mince a week ahead.

1 Make chocolate fruit mince.

2 Process flours, icing sugar and butter until mixture is crumbly. Add 1 egg and ¼ cup (60ml) chilled water; process until ingredients just come together. Turn dough onto floured surface, knead gently until smooth. Shape into a disc. Enclose with plastic wrap; refrigerate for 30 minutes.

3 Preheat oven to 180°C/350°F. Lightly grease two deep 12-hole (2-tablespoon/40ml) patty pans.

4 Roll two thirds of the chilled pastry between two sheets of baking paper until 3mm (⅛in) thick. Cut out 24 x 7cm (2¾in) rounds; press rounds into holes.

5 Divide chocolate fruit mince among pastry cases. Roll remaining pastry between two sheets of baking paper until 3mm (⅛in) thick. Cut out 24 x 5cm (2in) stars. Top pies with stars. Brush pastry with remaining beaten egg and sprinkle with demerara sugar.

6 Bake pies for 18 minutes or until browned. Leave pies in pans for 10 minutes; transfer, top-side up, onto a wire rack to cool.

chocolate fruit mince Combine ingredients in a large bowl. Cover tightly with plastic wrap. Refrigerate for up to a week; stirring mixture once a day. (Makes 3½ cups.)

KEEPING Filling can be made a week ahead. The pies will have a better flavour the longer you let then fruit mince stand.

PREP + COOK TIME 1 HOUR (+ STANDING & REFRIGERATION) **MAKES** 24

1½ cups (170g) quinoa flour
½ cup (60g) 100% corn (maize) cornflour (cornstarch)
½ cup (70g) gluten-free plain (all-purpose) flour
⅓ cup (55g) gluten-free icing (confectioners') sugar
100g (3oz) cold unsalted butter, chopped
2 eggs
2 tablespoons demerara sugar

CHOCOLATE FRUIT MINCE

1 cup (200g) dried figs, chopped
½ cup (85g) sultanas
½ cup (80g) currants
½ cup (85g) pitted prunes, chopped
150g (4½oz) dark chocolate (70% cocoa), processed finely
2 tablespoons brown sugar
½ teaspoon mixed spice
¼ teaspoon ground cloves
¼ cup (60ml) brandy
¼ cup (80g) fig jam

Chocolate mint LOAF CAKE

200g (6½oz) dark (70% cocoa) mint-flavoured chocolate
35g (1oz) peppermint crisp bar, coarsely chopped
500g (1lb) dark (semi-sweet) chocolate, chopped
600ml thickened (heavy) cream
dutch-processed cocoa, to dust

SPONGE CAKE

4 eggs
⅔ cup (150g) caster (superfine) sugar
⅓ cup (40g) 100% corn (maize) cornflour (cornstarch)
⅓ cup (45g) gluten-free self-raising flour
⅓ cup (45g) gluten-free plain (all-purpose) flour
1 tablespoon dutch-processed cocoa

1 Make sponge cake.

2 Grease a 10.5cm x 23cm (4in x 9in) (base measurement) 2 litre (8-cup) loaf pan; line base and sides with baking paper.

3 Place mint chocolate in a small heatproof bowl over a small saucepan of simmering water (don't let the water touch the base of the bowl); stir until smooth. Remove bowl from heat. Pour into lined pan; sprinkle peppermint crisp evenly over chocolate. Refrigerate for 15 minutes until just starting to set. Cut sponge cake into thirds crossways. Place a layer of cake on top of the chocolate base gently pressing to join together. Refrigerate.

4 Place the dark chocolate in a small heatproof bowl over a small saucepan of simmering water (don't let the water touch the base of the bowl); stir until smooth. Remove bowl from heat. Cool slightly.

5 Beat cream in a large bowl with an electric mixer until soft peaks form. Add the melted chocolate; beat until just combined.

6 Spoon one third of the mousse over the cake layer. Cover with another layer of cake then another third of the mousse, repeat layering finishing with the mousse; spread surface level. Refrigerate for 2 hours or overnight until set.

7 Remove from pan; dust top with cocoa. Serve cut into slices with a hot knife.

sponge cake Preheat oven to 180°C/350°F. Grease a deep 23cm (9in) square cake pan; line base with baking paper. Beat eggs and sugar in a large bowl with an electric mixer on high for 8 minutes or until mixture is thick and creamy. Triple sift flours and cocoa. Using a balloon whisk (or large metal spoon), fold flour mixture into egg mixture gently until just combined. Pour mixture into pan. Bake for 25 minutes or until cake is dry to the touch and edges are coming away from the sides of pan. Leave cake in pan for 5 minutes before turning, top-side up, onto a wire rack to cool.

NUT FREE

KEEPING Cake will keep refrigerated for up to 3 days.

PREP + COOK TIME 50 MINUTES (+ REFRIGERATION) **SERVES** 12

BAKED LEMON-ICED DOUGHNUTS
PAGES 196 & 197

Baked lemon-iced

DOUGHNUTS

YOU CAN DECORATE THE DOUGHNUTS WITH ALL MANNER OF TOPPINGS. WE HAVE CHOSEN A COMBINATION OF PISTACHIOS, ROSE PETALS, MIXED DRIED FLOWERS AND ORANGE SLICES, ALL AVAILABLE FROM HEALTH FOOD STORES AND SPECIALITY CAKE STORES. HOWEVER, YOU COULD ALSO USE FINELY GRATED LEMON OR ORANGE RIND, OR CHOPPED FREEZE-DRIED RASPBERRIES AND STRAWBERRY SLICES THAT ARE EASILY FOUND IN THE SNACK SECTION OF MOST MAJOR SUPERMARKETS.

1 Preheat oven to 180°C/350°F. Grease and flour a 6-hole (¼-cup/60ml) doughnut tray; shaking out excess flour.

2 Beat butter and sugar in a large bowl with an electric mixer until pale and creamy. Add eggs, one at a time, beating well after each addition. Add vanilla and almond extract. Combine almond meal, flour, baking powder and salt in a bowl. Add to butter mixture, alternating with milk, until smooth. Spoon some of the mixture into a disposable piping bag, snip end. Pipe mixture into doughnut tray, until each hole is three-quarters full.

3 Bake doughnuts for 15 minutes or until golden and a skewer inserted into the centre comes out clean. Leave doughnuts in pan for 3 minutes before turning, top-side up, onto wire racks to cool. Wash doughnut tray. Repeat greasing and flouring twice more, filling with remaining batter and baking to make 18 doughnuts in total.

4 Meanwhile, make lemon icing.

5 Dip doughnuts, one at a time, upside down into icing, Transfer to a wire rack. Scatter with the toppings of your choice. Stand for 10 minutes for icing to set.

lemon icing Combine sifted icing sugar and juice in a medium bowl. Adjust consistency with a little water, if necessary. Cover surface with plastic wrap; set aside until required.

TIPS If you like you can tint the lemon icing pastel colours, using pink and violet food colour. You can also bake the doughnut mixture in two greased and lined deep 20cm (8in) round cake pans for 45 minutes or until golden and a skewer inserted into the centre comes out clean. Leave cakes in pan for 10 minutes before, turning top-side up onto wire racks to cool. Drizzle cooled cakes with lemon icing.

PREP + COOK TIME 2 HOURS (+ REFRIGERATION) **MAKES** 18

375g (12oz) unsalted butter, at room temperature
2 cups (440g) caster (superfine) sugar
6 eggs
3 teaspoons vanilla bean paste
1½ teaspoons almond extract
1½ cups (180g) almond meal
3 cups (405g) gluten-free self-raising flour
1 teaspoon gluten-free baking powder
1 teaspoon fine sea salt
¾ cup (180ml) milk

LEMON ICING

4 cups (640g) gluten-free icing (confectioners') sugar mixture
⅓ cup (80ml) lemon juice

TOPPINGS

¼ cup (4g) dried rose petals
¼ cup (4g) mixed dried edible flowers
¼ cup (35g) coarsely chopped pistachios
3 dried orange slices, quartered

Persian LOVE CAKE

You will need to start this recipe a day ahead.

1 Make yoghurt icing.

2 Transfer yoghurt icing to a bowl. Reserve 1 cup of the whey (liquid) from drained yoghurt. Discard remaining whey.

3 Preheat oven to 160°C/325°F. Grease two deep 20cm (8in) round cake pans; line base and sides with baking paper.

4 Beat egg whites in a large bowl with an electric mixer until frothy. Add cream of tartar; beat to soft peaks. Gradually add sugar and beat until thick and glossy.

5 Whisk butter, egg yolks, rind and cardamom in a separate bowl until combined. Fold in almond meal and flour until combined.

6 Gently fold half the egg white mixture into almond mixture until just combined. Repeat with remaining egg white mixture. Divide mixture between pans; level surface.

7 Bake cakes for 50 minutes or until firm to the touch. Leave cakes in pans for 5 minutes before turning, top-side up, onto wire racks to cool.

8 Meanwhile, pour reserved whey into a small saucepan with honey and juice. Bring to the boil, add half each of the figs and rose petals. Reduce heat to medium; cook for 15 minutes or until syrup is reduced by a third. Cool to room temperature then refrigerate until cold. Strain syrup, pressing down lightly on figs to extract the flavour. Discard solids.

9 Using a serrated knife, cut each cake in half horizontally to create four even layers. Place one cake layer on a cake stand or serving plate. Brush with 2 tablespoons of the fig syrup. Spoon ¾ cup of the yoghurt icing onto cake layer on stand, spreading evenly using a offset palette knife. Repeat with remaining cake layers, syrup and icing.

10 Spread remaining icing over top and side of cake to create a thin see-through layer of icing. Refrigerate cake for 30 minutes or until firm. Serve topped with remaining figs and syrup, sprinkled with pistachios and remaining rose petals.

yoghurt icing Line a sieve with a clean tea towel or muslin cloth. Place yoghurt, sugar and rosewater in a large bowl; stir until well combined. Spoon mixture into lined sieve. Place sieve over a large bowl ensuring base of sieve is not touching base of bowl. Cover; refrigerate overnight.

PREP + COOK TIME 1 HOUR 45 MINUTES (+ COOLING & OVERNIGHT REFRIGERATION) **SERVES** 14

6 eggs, separated
½ teaspoon cream of tartar
1½ cups (330g) caster (superfine) sugar
250g (8oz) butter, melted, cooled
2 teaspoons finely grated lemon rind
1 teaspoon ground cardamom
3⅓ cups (400g) almond meal
1½ cups (200g) gluten-free self-raising flour
¾ cup (270g) honey
2 tablespoons lemon juice
6 figs (360g), halved
¼ cup (4g) dried rose petals
¼ cup (35g) coarsely chopped pistachios

YOGHURT ICING

2kg (4lb) greek yoghurt
½ cup (80g) gluten-free icing (confectioners') sugar
3 teaspoons rosewater

Pear & ginger CAKES

1 Make poached pears.

2 Preheat oven 160°C/325°F. Grease a 6-hole texas (¾-cup/180ml) muffin pan.

3 Combine butter, golden syrup and sugar in a large saucepan over medium heat; cook, stirring until butter melts and sugar dissolves. Remove pan from heat. Whisk in buttermilk, then egg. Sift flour, bicarb and spices over; stir until combined.

4 Spoon mixture into pan holes. Press a pear into the centre of each hole. Sprinkle with crystallised ginger.

5 Bake cakes for 35 minutes or until a skewer inserted into a cake comes out clean. Leave cakes in pan for 5 minutes before carefully lifting out onto plates. Serve drizzled with pear syrup.

poached pears Halve unpeeled pears, leaving stalks intact. Combine sugar, ginger and 2 cups (500ml) water in a medium saucepan over high heat; cook, stirring until sugar dissolves. Bring to the boil; add pears, simmer, covered, for 15 minutes or until just tender. Cool pears in syrup. Remove pears from syrup and place on several layers of paper towel to drain. Simmer syrup for 20 minutes until thickened; cool.

KEEPING Cakes are best eaten on the day they are made.

PREP + COOK TIME 1 HOUR 35 MINUTES **MAKES** 6

60g (2oz) butter
⅓ cup (90g) golden syrup
⅓ cup (75g) firmly packed brown sugar
¼ cup (60ml) buttermilk
1 egg
1¾ cups (235g) gluten-free self-raising flour
¼ teaspoon bicarbonate of soda (baking soda)
2 teaspoons ground ginger
1 teaspoon ground cinnamon
¼ teaspoon ground cardamom
2 tablespoons crystallised ginger, chopped finely

POACHED PEARS
3 buerre bosc pears (540g)
1 cup (220g) firmly packed brown sugar
1 teaspoon ground ginger

White chocolate & passionfruit ÉCLAIRS

1 Preheat oven to 200°C/400°F. Grease two oven trays; line with baking paper.
2 Stir butter and ⅔ cup (160ml) water in a medium saucepan over low heat until butter is melted. Bring to the boil. Add sifted flour and cream of tartar; cook, stirring vigorously for 30 seconds or until mixture forms a dough. Remove from heat.
3 Transfer mixture to a medium bowl of an electric mixer. Beat in eggs, one at a time, beating until well combined between additions.
4 Spoon mixture into a large piping bag fitted with a plain 2cm (¾in) round tube. Pipe 12 x 10cm (4in) lengths, 5cm (2in) apart, onto trays.
5 Bake éclairs for 30 minutes or until puffed and golden brown. Split éclairs lengthways; remove any soft dough from the centre. Return shells to trays; bake for a further 5 minutes to dry out shells. Cool.
6 Meanwhile, make white chocolate filling.
7 Just before serving, fill a small piping bag with the filling; cut a 1cm (½in) hole from the end of the bag. Pipe filling into éclair bases, drizzle with passionfruit; replace tops. Dust with icing sugar.

white chocolate filling Place chocolate and cream in a small microwave safe bowl; microwave on MEDIUM (50%), in 30-second bursts, stirring, until melted and smooth. Refrigerate for 1 hour or until cold. Beat cold mixture with an electric mixer on high until soft peaks form.

KKEEPING Unfilled éclairs can be made 2 days ahead. Store in an airtight container. Pipe filling into éclairs just before serving.

PREP + COOK TIME 1 HOUR 20 MINUTES (+ COOLING) **MAKES** 12

80g (3oz) butter
1 cup (135g) gluten-free plain (all-purpose) flour
1 teaspoon cream of tartar
4 eggs
1 passionfruit, pulp removed
1 tablespoon gluten-free icing (confectioners') sugar

WHITE CHOCOLATE FILLING
200g (6½oz) white chocolate, chopped coarsely
¾ cup (180ml) pouring cream

NUT FREE

Hazelnut, espresso & chocolate CHEESECAKE

1 Preheat oven to 160°C/325°F. Grease a 22cm (8¾in) round springform pan; line base and side with baking paper.

2 Make biscuit base. Firmly press biscuit mixture over base of pan with a straight-sided glass or bottle. Bake for 15 minutes or until dry to touch. Cool.

3 Meanwhile, process cream cheese, sugar and hazelnut spread in a food processor until smooth. Add sour cream, eggs, melted chocolate, espresso and cornflour; process until smooth. Pour mixture over base in pan. Lightly tap base of pan on bench top to release any air bubbles. Place pan on an oven tray.

4 Bake for 1 hour 15 minutes or until slightly risen around edge and still slightly wobbly in the centre. Remove from oven; cool for 30 minutes before refrigerating for 4 hours or until firm.

5 Meanwhile, make hazelnut brittle.

6 Combine chopped chocolate and 2 tablespoons boiling water in a small bowl. Microwave on LOW (20%) in 10-second bursts, stirring until melted. Beat cream in a bowl with an electric mixer until soft peaks form; fold through chocolate mixture.

7 Top cheesecake with brittle and black salt. Serve with chocolate cream.

biscuit base Place ingredients in a food processor bowl; pulse until fine crumbs form.

hazelnut brittle Line a large oven tray with baking paper. Place half the sugar in a medium saucepan over medium heat; cook, until sugar starts to melt around the edge. Cook, without stirring, for 6 minutes or a light caramel colour (time will depend on size of pan and stove). Add remaining sugar; cook for 4 minutes, swirling pan slightly until all the sugar has dissolved and caramel is golden. Working quickly, pour caramel onto lined tray; sprinkle with nuts. Cool. Chop coarsely.

KEEPING Cheesecake will keep refrigerated for up to 3 days.

PREP + COOK TIME 2 HOURS 10 MINUTES (+ REFRIGERATION & COOLING) **SERVES** 14

500g (1lb) cream cheese, softened
½ cup (110g) caster (superfine) sugar
400g (12½oz) chocolate-hazelnut spread
250g (8oz) sour cream
4 eggs
200g (6½oz) dark chocolate (70% cocoa), melted, cooled slightly
½ cup (125ml) espresso coffee
1 tablespoon 100% corn (maize) cornflour (cornstarch)
100g (3oz) dark chocolate (70% cocoa), chopped
300ml thickened (heavy) cream
black salt, optional, to serve

BISCUIT BASE

380g (12oz) gluten-free plain chocolate biscuits, broken into pieces
60g (2oz) butter, melted
2 tablespoons dutch-processed cocoa

HAZELNUT BRITTLE

1 cup (220g) caster (superfine) sugar
1 cup (135g) skinless roasted hazelnuts, chopped

You can... VARY THE FRUIT BASED ON WHAT'S IN SEASON. TRY SLICES OF MANGO BETWEEN THE LAYERS WITH A MIX OF MANGO, PINEAPPLE AND PASSIONFRUIT ON TOP, SPRINKLED WITH TOASTED FLAKED COCONUT INSTEAD OF HAZELNUTS.

Berry & coconut MERINGUE STACK

5 egg whites
½ teaspoon cream of tartar
1½ cups (330g) caster (superfine) sugar
⅔ cup (90g) skinless hazelnuts, roasted, chopped finely
1 cup (80g) desiccated coconut
⅓ cup (45g) skinless hazelnuts, halved, extra
2 tablespoons maple syrup
250g (8oz) strawberries
125g (4oz) blackberries
4 passionfruit, pulp removed

LEMON CREAM
2 egg yolks
¼ cup (55g) caster (superfine) sugar
3 teaspoons finely grated lemon rind
500g (1lb) sour cream
1 cup (250ml) pouring cream

1 Preheat oven to 120°C/250°F. Mark a 22cm (9in) circle on three pieces of baking paper; turn paper, marked-side down, on three oven trays.
2 Beat egg whites and cream of tartar in a large bowl with an electric mixer on high speed until soft peaks form. Gradually add sugar, beating after each addition until sugar is dissolved and mixture is glossy and firm. Gently fold in chopped hazelnuts and coconut. Spread mixture evenly among circles on trays.
3 Bake meringues for 1 hour or until firm and dry to touch. Turn off oven, leave meringues to cool in oven with door ajar.
4 Meanwhile, stir extra hazelnuts and maple syrup in a small non-stick frying pan over medium heat until sticky. Transfer to a plate lined with baking paper.
5 Make lemon cream.
6 Peel paper from meringues. Place one meringue layer on a cake plate or stand; spread with a third of the lemon cream, and top with a third of the strawberries. Repeat layering, finishing with lemon cream and strawberries; top with blackberries, candied hazelnuts and passionfruit. Serve immediately.

lemon cream Beat egg yolks, sugar and rind in a small bowl with an electric mixer for 5 minutes or until thick and pale. Add sour cream and cream, continue to whisk until soft peaks form. Refrigerate until required.

TIP If you can't buy skinless hazelnuts, roast whole hazelnuts in a 180°C/350°F oven for 8 minutes or until hazelnuts are golden brown and skins split. Tip hazelnuts onto a clean tea towel; rub hazelnuts firmly in towel to remove most of the skins.

KEEPING Meringue layers can be made a day ahead; store between baking paper in an airtight container. Assembled cake can be made to end of step 6 up to 4 hours ahead; keep refrigerated.

PREP + COOK TIME 1 HOUR 40 MINUTES (+ COOLING) **SERVES** 12

DAIRY FREE

NUT FREE

HOT CROSS BUNS

3 cups (405g) gluten-free plain (all-purpose) flour
½ cup (75g) potato flour
½ cup (80g) brown rice flour
½ cup (60g) tapioca flour
3 teaspoons mixed spice
1 teaspoon ground cinnamon
3 teaspoons (10g) dried yeast
2 teaspoons xanthan gum
¼ cup (55g) caster (superfine) sugar
3 egg whites
1 egg
¾ cup (180ml) olive oil
2 cups (500ml) milk
1 cup (160g) sultanas

FLOUR PASTE FOR CROSSES

½ cup (65g) gluten-free plain (all-purpose) flour
2 teaspoons caster (superfine) sugar

GLAZE

1 tablespoon caster (superfine) sugar
1 teaspoon gelatine

1 Grease a deep 23cm (9¼in) square cake pan.

2 Combine sifted flours, spices, yeast, xanthan gum and sugar in a large bowl.

3 Place egg whites, whole egg, oil and half the milk in a large bowl of an electric mixer; beat on medium speed for 3½ minutes. Add remaining milk and the flour mixture, 1 cup at a time, beating until combined and smooth. Fold through sultanas.

4 Divide dough into 16 pieces. With wet hands shape dough into balls. Place balls into pan; cover, stand in a warm place for 45 minutes.

5 Meanwhile, preheat oven to 220°C/425°F.

6 Make flour paste for crosses; place in a piping bag fitted with a small plain tube. Pipe crosses on buns.

7 Bake buns for 50 minutes, covering with foil after 30 minutes, or until golden and the buns sound hollow when tapped. Transfer buns, top-side up, onto a wire rack.

8 Make glaze; brush tops of hot buns with hot glaze. Serve buns warm.

flour paste for crosses Combine flour and sugar in a small bowl. Gradually blend in ⅓ cup (80ml) water, or enough water to form a smooth paste.

glaze Stir ingredients with 1 tablespoon water in a small saucepan over medium heat, without boiling, until sugar and gelatine dissolve.

TIPS Hot cross buns are best served warm on the day they are made. Buns can be reheated in the microwave on HIGH (100%) in 10-second bursts until heated through.

KEEPING Hot cross buns can be frozen for up to 1 month.

PREP + COOK TIME 1 HOUR 30 MINUTES (+ STANDING) **MAKES** 16

Scottish SHORTBREAD

1 Preheat oven to 150°C/300°F. Grease two oven trays; line with baking paper.
2 Beat butter and caster sugar in a small bowl with an electric mixer until just combined; gradually beat in the combined sifted flours, almond meal, icing sugar and xanthan gum until mixture starts to come together.
3 Turn dough onto a lightly rice-floured surface; knead until just smooth.
4 Divide dough into two portions. Shape portions into 18cm (7¼in) rounds on trays; mark into wedges, then prick with a fork. Pinch a decorative edge with floured fingers. Place in freezer for 15 minutes to chill.
5 Bake shortbread for 45 minutes or until pale golden. Cool shortbread rounds on trays. Cut with a sharp knife when cold.

KEEPING Shortbread can be made a month ahead; store in an airtight container.

PREP + COOK TIME 1 HOUR **MAKES** 16 WEDGES

250g (8oz) cold butter, chopped
½ cup (110g) caster (superfine) sugar
1¼ cups (225g) white rice flour
1½ cups (200g) gluten-free plain (all-purpose) flour
½ cups (60g) almond meal
⅓ cup (55g) gluten-free icing (confectioners') sugar
1 teaspoon xanthan gum

You can... SERVE THE PUDDING TOPPED WITH GOLDEN SYRUP AND A CROWN OF MUSCATELS ON THE VINE OR ACCOMPANY WITH A GLUTEN-FREE CUSTARD.

CHRISTMAS PUDDING

with brandy & ginger

You will need to start this recipe a day ahead.

1 Combine dried fruit and brandy in a large bowl. Cover; refrigerate overnight or longer if time permits.

2 Grease two 1.5 litre (6-cup) pudding basins or steamers. Line bases with a small round of baking paper. Place a 30cm x 40cm (12in x 16in) piece of baking paper on top of a piece of foil cut the same size; fold a 5cm (2in) pleat crossways through the centre. Repeat to make two.

3 Beat eggs and sugar in a small bowl with electric mixer on high for 8 minutes or until thick and pale. Stir in dried fruit mixture with apple, rind, juice, butter, breadcrumbs and mixed spice until combined.

4 Spoon mixture evenly into basins, topping puddings with the pleated baking paper and foil, paper-side down (this allows puddings to expand as they cook); secure well with kitchen string (or lid).

5 Place an inverted saucer on the base of two large saucepans; place pudding basins on each saucer. Pour enough boiling water into pans to come halfway up the side of the basins; cover with tight-fitting lids. Boil puddings for 5 hours, replenishing with boiling water as necessary to maintain water level.

6 Remove puddings from water. Stand for 5 minutes before turning out.

TIP If you only wish to make one pudding, halve the recipe.

KEEPING Puddings can be cooked ahead of time and reheated in steamers for 1 hour on the day of serving. Store puddings wrapped in plastic in the refrigerator, for up to 3 months or freeze.

PREP + COOK TIME 5 HOURS 30 MINUTES (+ REFRIGERATION)
SERVES 16 (MAKES 2 PUDDINGS)

350g (11oz) raisins
150g (4½oz) dried apricots, chopped
350g (11oz) sultanas
150g (4½oz) dried figs, chopped
100g (3oz) glacé ginger, chopped
⅔ cup (160ml) brandy
6 eggs
1 cup (160g) coconut sugar
2 medium apples (300g), grated coarsely
1½ tablespoons finely grated orange rind
¼ cup (60ml) orange juice
250g (8oz) butter, melted
1½ cups (195g) gluten-free breadcrumbs
2 teaspoons mixed spice

ORANGE CAKE
WITH LABNE
PAGES 216 & 217

ORANGE CAKE *with labne*

LABNE IS MADE BY STRAINING YOGHURT THROUGH A FINE CLOTH TO RELEASE THE LIQUID COMPONENT, WHICH IS KNOWN AS WHEY. THE LONGER THE STRAINING TIME, THE THICKER THE LABNE WILL BECOME. THE LEFTOVER WHEY WILL KEEP REFRIGERATED FOR UP TO 2 DAYS. USE IT IN YOUR SMOOTHIES OR SOUPS.
A SAVOURY LABNE CAN BE MADE BY OMITTING THE SUGAR AND VANILLA. TO FAST TRACK THE DRAINING PROCESS, WRING THE TOP OF THE CLOTH EVERY 15 MINUTES.

You will need to start the labne a day ahead.

1 Make vanilla labne.

2 Preheat oven 160°C/325°F. Grease a deep 20cm (8in) round cake pan; line base and side with baking paper.

3 Whisk egg whites, butter, almond meal, icing sugar, sifted flour, rind and nutmeg in a large bowl until well combined. Pour mixture into pan.

4 Bake cake for 1 hour 40 minutes (cover with foil halfway through cooking to prevent overbrowning) or until a skewer inserted in the centre comes out clean. Leave cake in pan for 10 minutes before turning, top-side up, onto a wire rack over an oven tray.

5 Meanwhile, remove rind from oranges in long strips with a zester. Squeeze juice from oranges; you need ½ cup (125ml) juice. Stir orange and lemon juices, caster sugar and strips of orange rind in a small saucepan over medium heat until sugar dissolves. Bring to the boil; boil for 5 minutes or until syrup thickens. Remove from heat. Reserve 2 tablespoons syrup and rind. Pour remaining hot syrup over hot cake.

6 Serve cooled cake with vanilla labne and reserved syrup and rind.

vanilla labne Stir ingredients in a medium bowl until combined. Spoon yoghurt mixture into a sieve lined with two layers of muslin (or a clean Chux cloth); place over a medium bowl. Tie cloth close to yoghurt. Refrigerate for 4 hours or overnight, twisting the yoghurt ball at the top occasionally, or until thick. Stir labne until smooth.

PREP + COOK TIME 2 HOURS (+ REFRIGERATION & STANDING)
SERVES 8

9 egg whites
270g (8½oz) butter, melted
1½ cups (180g) almond meal
2¼ cups (360g) gluten-free icing (confectioners') sugar
¾ cup (100g) gluten-free plain (all-purpose) flour
2 teaspoons finely grated orange rind
½ teaspoon ground nutmeg
2 oranges (480g)
¼ cup (60ml) lemon juice
1½ cups (330g) caster (superfine) sugar

VANILLA LABNE

1 teaspoon vanilla bean paste
1kg (2lb) greek yoghurt
½ teaspoon sea salt flakes
2 tablespoons caster (superfine) sugar

GINGERBREAD *houses*

125g (4oz) butter, softened
½ cup (175g) golden syrup (or treacle)
½ cup (110g) firmly packed dark brown sugar
2½ cups (335g) gluten-free plain (all-purpose) flour
1 tablespoon ground ginger
1 teaspoon ground cinnamon
¼ teaspoon ground cloves
1 tablespoon xanthan gum
gluten-free icing (confectioners') sugar, for dusting

ROYAL ICING
1½ cups (240g) gluten-free icing (confectioners') sugar
1 egg white
1 teaspoon lemon juice

NUT FREE

1 Using templates from page 240, trace and cut out the shapes using firm cardboard.

2 Beat butter, golden syrup and sugar in a medium bowl with an electric mixer until creamy and pale in colour. Add combined sifted flour, spices and xanthan gum; stir until mixture just comes together. Knead dough gently on a surface lightly dusted with gluten-free flour until smooth. Enclose with plastic wrap; refrigerate 30 minutes or until firm.

3 Preheat oven to 180°C/350°F. Grease two oven trays; line with baking paper.

4 To make side walls: roll one-third of the dough on a surface dusted with gluten-free flour until 3mm (⅛in) thick. Using wall template, cut out 16 squares; place 3cm (1¼in) apart on trays.

5 Bake for 10 minutes or until lightly golden. Slide paper and gingerbread walls from trays onto a wire rack to cool. Cool and re-line trays.

6 To make front and back walls: repeat with rolling half the remaining dough. Using end wall template, cut out 16 walls; place on trays. Bake as per instructions in step 5.

7 To make roofs: repeat rolling remaining dough. Using the roof template, cut out 16 rectangles; place on trays. Bake as per instructions in step 5.

8 Make royal icing. Fill piping bag fitted with a fine piping nozzle (no. 2). Pipe icing onto sides of shapes, attaching side walls with front and back walls to make a house (hold in place for a few minutes to stabilise, if necessary). Pipe along the top edge with a little icing; position roof (hold in position, if necessary). Repeat with remaining pieces to make a total of 8 houses. Stand for 30 minutes or until icing is set.

9 Using picture as a guide decorate houses with royal icing. Stand for 30 minutes or until set. Dust with icing sugar.

royal icing Sift icing sugar through a fine sieve into a bowl. Lightly beat egg white in a small bowl with an electric mixer until it is just broken up – do not whip into peaks. Beat in the icing sugar, a tablespoon at a time, to reach the required consistency. When icing reaches right consistency, stir in juice. Cover surface directly with plastic wrap until ready to use.

KEEPING Gingerbread houses will keep in an airtight container for up to 1 week.

PREP + COOK TIME 2 HOURS (+ REFRIGERATION & STANDING)
MAKES 8

Coconut & hazelnut CAKE

1 Preheat oven to 160°C/325°F. Grease a deep 23cm (9in) round springform cake pan. Line base and side with baking paper.

2 Combine hazelnut meal, desiccated coconut and baking powder in a large bowl. Whisk eggs and sugar in a medium bowl with an electric mixer on high speed for 5 minutes or until thick. Fold in melted butter then hazelnut mixture. Pour mixture into lined pan.

3 Bake for 35 minutes or until just firm to touch. Cover with foil if over browning. Cool in pan.

4 Make blistered grapes.

5 Serve cake topped with blistered grapes and syrup.

blistered grapes Preheat oven grill (broiler) to high. Line a large oven tray with foil. Place grapes on tray; top with sugar, honey, cinnamon sticks, lemon juice and 2 tablespoons water. Cook under the grill for 15 minutes or until grapes are blistered and juices are beginning to thicken. Cool.

KEEPING Cake will keep for 3 days without grapes and syrup; store at room temperature in an airtight container.

PREP + COOK TIME 55 MINUTES **SERVES** 8

2 cups (200g) hazelnut meal
1 cup (80g) desiccated coconut
½ teaspoon gluten-free baking powder
4 eggs
¾ cup (165g) firmly packed brown sugar
100g (3oz) butter, melted, cooled

BLISTERED GRAPES

200g (6½oz) red grapes
½ cup (55g) caster (superfine) sugar
¼ cup (180g) honey
2 cinnamon sticks
1 tablespoon lemon juice

BOILED PUDDINGS
PAGES 224 & 225

Boiled PUDDINGS

YOU WILL NEED 6 X 35CM (14IN) SQUARES UNBLEACHED CALICO FOR THE BOILED PUDDING CLOTHS. IF CALICO HAS NOT BEEN USED BEFORE, YOU WILL NEED TO SOAK IT OVERNIGHT IN COLD WATER. THE NEXT DAY, BOIL IT FOR 20 MINUTES, THEN RINSE THE CLOTH IN COLD WATER. TO FREEZE PUDDINGS, WRAP THEM TIGHTLY IN PLASTIC WRAP, SEAL TIGHTLY IN A FREEZER BAG OR AIRTIGHT CONTAINER, AND STORE IN THE FRIDGE FOR 1 MONTH OR FREEZER FOR 3 MONTHS.

You will need to start this recipe a day ahead.

1 Combine mixed fruit, apple, liqueur, rind, mixed spice and cinnamon in a large bowl. Cover with plastic wrap; stand at room temperature overnight.

2 Beat butter and sugar in a small bowl with an electric mixer until pale. Beat in eggs, one at a time. Stir egg mixture into fruit mixture. Add breadcrumbs and combined sifted flours; stir to combine.

3 Fill a boiler three quarters full of hot water, cover with a tight fitting lid; bring to the boil. Have ready 1 metre (3 feet) of kitchen string, plus extra gluten-free flour. Wearing thick rubber gloves and using tongs, dip pudding cloths, one at a time, into boiling water; boil for 1 minute, then remove. Squeeze excess water from cloth. Spread hot cloths on bench; rub 2 tablespoons of the extra flour into centre of each cloth to cover an area about 20cm (8in) in diameter, leaving flour a little thicker in centre of cloth where "skin" of the pudding needs to be thickest. Divide pudding mixture equally among cloths, placing in centre of each cloth. Gather cloths around mixture, avoiding any deep pleats; pat into round shapes. Tie cloths tightly with string, as close to mixture as possible. Tie loops in string. Lower three puddings into boiling water. Cover; boil for 2 hours, replenishing with boiling water as necessary to maintain the water level in the boiler.

4 Lift puddings from water, one at a time, using wooden spoons through string loops. Do not put pudding on bench; suspend from spoon by placing over rungs of an upturned stool or wedging the spoon in a drawer. Twist ends of cloth around string to avoid them touching pudding; hang for 10 minutes. Repeat with remaining puddings.

5 Place puddings on board; cut string, carefully peel back cloth. Turn puddings onto plate, then carefully peel cloth away completely. Stand 20 minutes or until skin darkens and pudding becomes firm.

6 Serve puddings with store-bought gluten-free custard and maple syrup, if you like.

PREP + COOK TIME 2 HOURS 30 MINUTES **MAKES** 6

1kg (2lb) dried mixed fruit
1 large fresh apple (200g), grated coarsely
½ cup (125ml) orange-flavoured liqueur
1 tablespoon finely grated orange rind
2 teaspoons mixed spice
2 teaspoons ground cinnamon
125g (4oz) butter, softened
½ cup (110g) firmly packed dark brown sugar
2 eggs
2 cups (140g) stale gluten-free white breadcrumbs
½ cup (60g) tapioca flour
1 cup (135g) gluten-free plain (all-purpose) flour
6 x 35cm (14in) squares unbleached calico (see note opposite)

NUT FREE

NUT FREE

Red velvet MUD CAKE

500g (1lb) butter, chopped
300g (9½oz) white chocolate, chopped
4 cups (880g) caster (superfine) sugar
2 teaspoons vanilla extract
2 cups (500ml) milk
2 cups (270g) gluten-free plain (all-purpose) flour
1½ cups (200g) gluten-free self-raising flour
½ cup (90g) buckwheat flour
1 cup (80g) gluten-free baby rice cereal
2 tablespoons cocoa powder
6 eggs
¼ cup (60ml) liquid red food colouring
125g (4oz) raspberries
gluten-free icing (confectioners') sugar, to dust

CREAM CHEESE FROSTING
80g (2½oz) butter, softened
200g (6½oz) cream cheese, softened
¼ teaspoon vanilla extract
4 cups (640g) gluten-free icing (confectioners') sugar

1 Preheat oven to 180°C/350°F. Grease three deep 22cm (9in) round cake pans; line bases and sides with baking paper.

2 Stir butter, chocolate, sugar, vanilla and milk in a large saucepan, over low heat until butter and chocolate are melted and mixture is smooth. Cool for 10 minutes.

3 Combine sifted flours, rice cereal and cocoa in a large bowl; gradually whisk in combined eggs and cooled chocolate mixture with food colouring. Divide mixture evenly among pans.

4 Bake cakes for 1 hour or until a skewer inserted into the centre comes out clean. Cool cakes in pans.

5 Meanwhile, make cream cheese frosting.

6 Place one cake on a serving plate or cake stand, spread with 1 cup of the frosting. Layer with second cake and another cup of frosting. Finish with third cake and remaining frosting. Top with raspberries and dust with icing sugar.

cream cheese frosting Beat butter, cream cheese and vanilla in a small bowl with an electric mixer for 2 minutes until smooth. Add sifted icing sugar, 1 cup at a time, beating well between additions. Scrape down sides of bowl and beat for a further 1 minute or until light and fluffy.

KEEPING Cake will keep for up to 3 days in an airtight container in the refrigerator.

PREP + COOK TIME 1 HOUR 20 MINUTES (+ COOLING) **SERVES** 12

DAIRY FREE

Glacé fruit Christmas CAKE

1½ cups (240g) sultanas
¾ cup (125ml) mixed peel
⅔ cup (140g) glacé cherries, quartered
½ cup (115g) coarsely chopped glacé pineapple
⅔ cup (150g) coarsely chopped dried juicy apricots
½ cup (115g) coarsely chopped glacé ginger
½ cup (125ml) Cointreau or other orange-flavoured liqueur
250g (8oz) dairy-free spread
1¼ cups (250g) firmly packed brown sugar
½ cup (125ml) soy milk
1 cup (135g) gluten-free plain (all-purpose) flour
1 cup (135g) gluten-free self-raising flour
1 cup (120g) almond meal
½ teaspoon bicarbonate of soda (baking soda)
1 teaspoon ground cinnamon
4 eggs, beaten lightly

1 Preheat oven to 150°C/300°F. Oil a deep 20cm (8in) round cake pan; line base and side with three layers of baking paper, extending the papers 5cm (2in) above the side.

2 Combine dried fruit and ¼ cup (60ml) Cointreau in a large bowl.

3 Stir dairy-free spread, sugar and soy milk in a medium saucepan over low heat until sugar dissolves; pour over fruit mixture. Stir sifted dry ingredients into fruit mixture, in two batches, until combined. Stir in egg.

4 Spread mixture evenly into pan. Tap pan firmly on the bench to settle the mixture; smooth the surface.

5 Bake cake for 2½ hours or until cooked when tested (insert the blade of a sharp pointed knife gently through the centre of the cake to the bottom of the pan; gently withdraw the knife, there should be no uncooked mixture on the blade). If necessary, cover the cake with foil during cooking to prevent over browning.

6 Brush hot cake with remaining liqueur. Cover hot cake with foil; cool in pan overnight. Serve decorated with extra glacé fruit, if desired.

TIP Replace liqueur with orange juice, if you prefer.

KEEPING Cake will keep for up to 2 weeks in an airtight container in the refrigerator, or freeze for up to 3 months.

PREP + COOK TIME 3 HOURS (+ COOLING) **SERVES** 12

BUTTERMILK CHOCOLATE CAKE

with white chocolate ganache

250g (8oz) butter, chopped coarsely
200g (6½oz) dark (semi-sweet) chocolate, chopped coarsely
2 cups (440g) caster (superfine) sugar
2 teaspoons vanilla extract
1 cup (250ml) buttermilk
1 cup (135g) gluten-free plain (all-purpose) flour
1 cup (135g) gluten-free self-raising flour
¾ cup (90g) almond meal
⅓ cup (35g) cocoa powder
½ teaspoon fine salt
2 eggs

WHITE CHOCOLATE GANACHE
300g (9½oz) white chocolate, chopped coarsely
1 cup (250ml) thickened (heavy) cream

1 Grease a deep 22cm (9in) round cake pan; line base and side with baking paper.
2 Stir butter, chocolate, sugar and vanilla in a large saucepan over low heat for 5 minutes or until chocolate melts and mixture is smooth. Remove from heat; stir in buttermilk. Cool for 5 minutes.
3 Whisk sifted flours, almond meal, cocoa and salt into chocolate mixture. Add eggs, whisk until combined. Pour mixture into pan; stand for 30 minutes.
4 Meanwhile, preheat oven to 160°C/325°F.
5 Bake cake for 1½ hours. Cool in pan.
6 Meanwhile, make white chocolate ganache.
7 Place cake on a serving plate or cake stand; spread ganache over top of cake.

white chocolate ganache Place chocolate and cream in a small heatproof bowl over a small saucepan of simmering water (don't let the water touch the base of the bowl); stir until chocolate melts and mixture is smooth. Refrigerate, stirring occasionally, for 30 minutes or until ganache is of a spreadable consistency.

KEEPING Cake will keep with or without chocolate ganache for up to 3 days.

PREP + COOK TIME 1 HOUR 45 MINUTES (+ STANDING & COOLING)
SERVES 16

You can... USE READY-MIXED DRIED FRUIT OR USE OUR CUSTOM SUGGESTION OF 150G (4OZ) EACH: CURRANTS, SULTANAS, PITTED FRESH DATES AND 300G (9OZ) DRIED FIGS, CHOPPED FINELY, FOR THE PUDDING.

Steamed Christmas PUDDING

You will need to start the fruit mixture a day ahead.

1 Combine mixed fruit, apple, sherry, rind, mixed spice and cinnamon in a large bowl. Cover with plastic wrap; stand at room temperature overnight.

2 Grease a 2 litre (8-cup) pudding basin or steamer with a little dairy-free spread. Line base with a small round of baking paper. Arrange the clementine slices in the base of the pan in a circular pattern, slightly overlapping each other. Place a 30cm x 40cm (12in x 16in) piece of baking paper on top of a piece of foil cut to the same size; fold a 5cm (2in) pleat crossways through the centre.

3 Beat spread and sugar in a small bowl with an electric mixer until pale. Beat in eggs, one at a time. Stir egg mixture into fruit mixture. Add breadcrumbs and combined sifted flours; stir to combine. Spoon mixture into basin; top with the pleated baking paper and foil, paper-side down (this allows the pudding to expand as it cooks); secure with kitchen string (or the lid).

4 Place an inverted saucer in the base of a large saucepan; place pudding basin on the saucer. Pour enough boiling water into the pan to come halfway up the side of the basin; cover with a tight-fitting lid. Boil pudding for 6 hours, replenishing with boiling water as necessary to maintain water level.

5 Remove pudding basin from water. Stand pudding for 10 minutes before turning out. Serve pudding topped with a sprig of thyme and drizzled with golden syrup.

750g (1½lb) dried mixed fruit (see above)
1 large apple (200g), grated coarsely
½ cup (125ml) dry sherry, port or pedro ximénez
1 tablespoon finely grated orange rind
2 teaspoons mixed spice
1 teaspoon ground cinnamon
3 candied clementines, sliced
125g (4oz) dairy-free spread
½ cup (110g) firmly packed brown sugar
2 eggs
2 cups (140g) stale gluten-free breadcrumbs
½ cup (65g) gluten-free plain (all-purpose) flour
½ cup (60g) tapioca flour
sprig of thyme and golden syrup, to serve

KEEPING Pudding can be made 1 week ahead; store, covered, in the fridge, or freeze for up to 3 months. To reheat frozen pudding, thaw for 3 days in the fridge; remove from fridge 12 hours before reheating. Discard plastic wrap and return pudding to pudding basin. Steam for 2 hours following instructions in step 4.

PREP + COOK TIME 7 HOURS (+ STANDING) **SERVES** 12

DAIRY FREE
NUT FREE

GLOSSARY

ALLSPICE so-named because it tastes like a combination of cumin, nutmeg, clove and cinnamon. Available whole or ground.

ALMONDS flat, pointy-tipped nuts with a pitted brown shell enclosing a creamy white kernel that is covered by a brown skin.

flaked paper-thin slices.

meal also known as ground almonds.

slivered small pieces cut lengthways.

BAKING PAPER also called parchment or baking parchment; a silicone-coated paper used primarily for lining baking pans and oven trays, so cakes and biscuits won't stick, making removal easy.

BAKING POWDER, GLUTEN-FREE a raising agent; readily available from supermarkets.

BICARBONATE OF SODA (BAKING SODA) a raising agent.

BLIND BAKING a cooking term to describe baking a pie shell or pastry case before filling is added. If a filling does not need to be baked or is very wet, you may need to 'blind-bake' the unfilled shell first. To bake blind, ease the pastry into a pan or dish, place on an oven tray; line the pastry with baking paper, then fill with dried beans, uncooked rice or pie weights. Bake according to the recipe, then cool before adding the filling.

BUTTER we use salted butter unless stated otherwise in the recipe; 125g is equal to 1 stick (4oz).

BUTTERMILK originally the term given to the slightly sour liquid left after butter was churned from cream, today it is made from no-fat or low-fat milk to which specific bacterial cultures have neen added. Despite its name, it is actually low in fat.

CACAO

nibs can be separated into cocoa butter and powder. Cocoa powder retains many beneficial antioxidants and is an easy way of adding cocoa into your diet without the kilojoules of chocolate.

powder is made by removing the cocoa butter using a process known as cold-pressing. It retains more of its nutrients than heat-processed cacao powder; it also has a stronger, slightly bitter, taste.

CARDAMOM a spice native to India and used extensively in its cuisine; can be purchased in pod, seed or ground form. Has a distinctive aromatic, sweetly rich flavour.

CHEESE

blue mould-treated cheeses mottled with blue veining. Varieties include firm, crumbly stilton types and mild, creamy brie-like cheeses.

bocconcini from the diminutive of boccone meaning mouthful, is the term used for walnut-sized, baby mozzarella, a delicate, semi-soft, white cheese traditionally made in Italy from buffalo milk. Spoils rapidly so must be refrigerated, in brine, for 1 or 2 days at most.

cheddar the most common cow's milk 'tasty' cheese; should be aged, hard and have a pronounced bite.

cream commonly called philadelphia or philly; a soft cow-milk cheese, its fat content ranges from 14 to 33%.

fetta Greek in origin; a crumbly textured goat or sheep milk cheese with a sharp, salty taste. Ripened and stored in salted whey.

goat's made from goat's milk, has an earthy, strong taste; available in both soft and firm textures, in various shapes and sizes, and sometimes rolled in ash or herbs.

gruyère a hard-rind Swiss cheese with small holes and a nutty, slightly salty flavour.

haloumi a Greek Cypriot cheese with a semi-firm, spongy texture and very salty sweet flavour. Ripened and stored in salted whey; best grilled or fried, it holds its shape well on being heated. Eat while still warm as it becomes rubbery on cooling.

mascarpone an Italian fresh cultured-cream product made in much the same way as yoghurt. Whiteish to creamy yellow in colour, with a buttery-rich, luscious texture.

parmesan also called parmigiano; is a hard, grainy cow-milk cheese originating in Italy.

ricotta a soft, sweet, moist, white cow-milk cheese with a low fat content and a slightly grainy texture. The name roughly translates as 'cooked again' and refers to ricotta's manufacture from a whey that is itself a by-product of other cheese making.

CHIA SEEDS contain protein, all the essential amino acids and a wealth of vitamins, minerals and antioxidants, as well as being fibre-rich.

CHICKPEAS (GARBANZO BEANS) also called hummus or channa; an irregularly round, sandy-coloured legume. Has a firm texture even after cooking, with a floury mouth-feel and robust nutty flavour; available canned or dried.

CHOCOLATE

dairy-free dark buy a high-quality dark chocolate, which should only contain cocoa butter, cocoa liquor, lecithin (usually soy-based) and sugar. It should not contain any milk products; always check the ingredient label.

dark (semi-sweet) also called luxury chocolate; made of a high percentage of cocoa liquor and cocoa butter, and little added sugar.

melts small discs of compounded milk, white or dark chocolate ideal for melting and moulding.

white contains no cocoa solids but is a mixture of cocoa butter, milk solids and sugar. It is very sensitive to heat.

CHOCOLATE-HAZELNUT SPREAD also known as Nutella; made of cocoa powder, hazelnuts, sugar and milk.

COCOA POWDER also called cocoa; dried, unsweetened, roasted and ground cocoa beans (cacao seeds).
dutch-processed is treated with an alkali to neutralise its acids. It has a reddish-brown colour, a mild flavour and is easy to dissolve.
COCONUT
cream obtained commercially from the first pressing of the coconut flesh alone, without the addition of water; the second pressing (less rich) is sold as coconut milk. Available in cans and cartons at most supermarkets.
desiccated concentrated, dried, unsweetened and finely shredded coconut flesh.
flaked dried flaked coconut flesh.
shredded unsweetened thin strips of dried coconut flesh.
CORIANDER (CILANTRO) also called pak chee or chinese parsley; bright-green-leafed herb with both pungent aroma and taste. Both the stems and roots of coriander are used in cooking: wash well before chopping. Coriander seeds are dried and sold either whole or ground, and neither form tastes remotely like the fresh leaf.
CORNFLOUR (CORNSTARCH) thickening agent available in two forms: 100% corn (maize), which is gluten free, and a wheaten cornflour (made from wheat) which is not.
CREAM
pouring also called pure or fresh cream. It contains no additives and has a minimum fat content of 35%.
sour a thick, commercially-cultured sour cream with a minimum fat content of 35%.
thick (double) a dolloping cream with a minimum fat content of 45%.
thickened (heavy) a whipping cream that contains a thickener. It has a minimum fat content of 35%.
CREAM OF TARTAR the acid ingredient in baking powder; added to confectionery mixtures to help prevent sugar from crystallising. Keeps frostings creamy and improves volume when beating egg whites.
CRÈME FRAÎCHE a mature, naturally fermented cream (minimum fat content 35%), with a velvety texture and slightly tangy, nutty flavour. It can be boiled without curdling.
DAIRY-FREE SPREAD made from vegetable oils; dairy-free substitute for butter.
FLOUR
arrowroot a starch made from the rhizome of a Central American plant, used mostly as a thickening agent.
buckwheat not actually a form of wheat, but a herb in the same plant family as rhubarb; is gluten-free. Has a strong nutty taste.
chickpea (besan) also called gram; made from ground chickpeas so is gluten free and high in protein.
gluten-free plain (all-purpose) a blend of gluten-free flours and starches (may include corn, potato, tapioca, chickpea and rice).
gluten-free self-raising made similarly to gluten-free plain flour, but with the addition of gluten-free bicarbonate of soda (baking soda).
potato made from cooked, dehydrated and ground potato; not to be confused with potato starch which is made from starch only. Has a strong potato flavour and is a heavy flour so a little goes a long way.
rice very fine, almost powdery, gluten-free flour; made from ground white rice.
tapioca made from the root of the cassava plant; a soft, fine, light white flour.
FOOD COLOURING vegetable-based substance available in liquid, paste or gel form. Available from major supermarkets and cake decorating suppliers.
GELATINE a thickening agent; available dried (powdered) gelatine and in sheets (leaf) gelatine. Three teaspoons of dried gelatine (8g) equals about four leaves. The two types are interchangeable but leaf gelatine gives a much clearer mixture than the powder. For titanium-strength gelatine, it is more accurate to follow the weight directed in the recipe rather than the number of sheets.
GINGER
fresh also called green or root ginger; the thick gnarled root of a tropical plant.
glacé fresh ginger root preserved in sugar syrup; crystallised ginger (sweetened with cane sugar) can be substituted if rinsed with warm water and dried before using.
ground also called powdered ginger; used as a flavouring in baking but cannot be substituted for fresh ginger.
GLACÉ FRUIT fruit such as pineapple, apricots, peaches and pears that are cooked in a heavy sugar syrup then dried.
GLUCOSE SYRUP also known as liquid glucose; used in jam and confectionery making.
HAZELNUTS also known as filberts; plump, grape-sized, rich, sweet nuts with a brown skin that is removed by rubbing heated nuts together vigorously in a tea towel.
meal also called ground hazelnuts; is made by grinding the hazelnuts to a coarse flour texture for use in baking or as a thickening agent.
KAFFIR LIME LEAVES also called bai magrood; looks like two glossy dark green leaves joined end to end, forming a rounded hourglass shape. Dried leaves are less potent, so double the number called for in a recipe if you substitute them for fresh. A strip of fresh lime peel may be substituted for each kaffir lime leaf.
LEMON CURD, GLUTEN-FREE a smooth spread, usually made from lemons, butter and eggs.

MAPLE SYRUP, PURE distilled from the sap of sugar maple trees found only in Canada and the USA. Maple-flavoured syrup or pancake syrup is not an adequate substitute for the real thing.
MISO fermented soybean paste. There are many types of miso, each with its own aroma, flavour, colour and texture; it can be kept, airtight, for up to a year in the fridge. Generally, the darker the miso, the saltier the taste and denser the texture. Buy in tubs or plastic packs.
MIXED PEEL candied citrus peel.
MIXED SPICE a classic spice mixture generally containing caraway, allspice, coriander, cumin, nutmeg and ginger, although cinnamon and other spices can be added. It is used with fruit and in cakes.
MUSLIN a loosely-woven cotton fabric used to separate liquid from solids. You could also use a clean Chux cloth.
NUTMEG a strong and pungent spice ground from the dried nut of an evergreen tree native to Indonesia. Usually found ground but the flavour is more intense from a whole nut; available from spice shops, so it's best to grate your own.
OIL
coconut is extracted from the coconut flesh so you don't get any of the fibre, protein or carbohydrates present in the whole coconut. The best quality is virgin coconut oil, which is the oil pressed from the dried coconut flesh, and doesn't include the use of solvents or other refining processes.
olive made from ripened olives. Extra virgin and virgin are the first and second press, respectively, of the olives and are therefore considered the best; 'light' refers to taste not fat levels.
vegetable oils sourced from plants.
ONION
green (scallion) also known as (incorrectly) shallot; an immature onion picked before the bulb has formed, with a long, bright green edible stalk.
red also known as spanish, red spanish or bermuda onion; a sweet-flavoured, large, purple-red onion that is particularly good eaten raw in salads.
ORANGE FLOWER WATER concentrated flavouring made from orange blossoms. Available from Middle-Eastern food stores and some delicatessens. Cannot be substituted with citrus flavourings, as the taste is completely different.
PASTRY, GLUTEN-FREE made from a blend of gluten-free flours and starches (may include corn, rice, tapioca, potato starch, pea) and binding and raising agents. Available in health-food stores, and in the health-food section of most supermarkets.
POLENTA also called cornmeal; a flourlike cereal made of dried corn (maize) sold ground in different textures; also the name of the dish made from it.
POMEGRANATE MOLASSES not to be confused with pomegranate syrup or grenadine which is used in cocktails; pomegranate molasses is thicker, browner and more concentrated in flavour, tart and sharp, slightly sweet and fruity. Buy from Middle Eastern food stores or specialty food shops.
QUINOA pronounced keen-wa; is the seed of a leafy plant similar to spinach. It has a delicate, slightly nutty taste and chewy texture.
flakes the grains have been rolled and flattened.
RICE CEREAL, GLUTEN-FREE BABY made from ground rice and sunflower oil; always check the packaging as some may also contain traces of wheat, milk and soy.
ROSEWATER extract made from crushed rose petals, called gulab in India; used for its aromatic quality in many sweetmeats and desserts.
SUGAR
brown a very soft, finely granulated sugar retaining molasses for its characteristic colour and flavour.
caster (superfine) finely granulated table sugar; dissolves easily.
coconut not made from coconuts, but the sap of the blossoms of the coconut palm tree. The refined sap looks a little like raw or light brown sugar, and has a similar caramel flavour. It also has the same amount of kilojoules as regular white (granulated) sugar.
demerara small-grained golden-coloured crystal sugar.
icing (confectioners') also called powdered sugar; pulverised granulated sugar crushed together with a small amount of cornflour (cornstarch).
raw natural brown granulated sugar.
TAHINI a rich, sesame-seed paste; available from health food stores and supermarkets.
TAMARI a thick, dark soy sauce made mainly from soy beans and without the wheat used in standard soy sauce.
VANILLA
extract obtained from vanilla beans infused in water; a non-alcoholic version of essence.
paste made from vanilla beans and contains real seeds. Is highly concentrated: 1 teaspoon replaces a whole vanilla bean.
XANTHAN GUM is a thickening agent produced by fermentation of, usually, corn sugar. When buying xanthan gum, ensure the packet states 'made from fermented corn sugar'. Found in the health-food section in larger supermarkets.
YEAST (DRIED AND FRESH) a raising agent used in dough making. Granular (7g sachets) and fresh compressed (20g blocks) yeast can almost always be substituted for the other when yeast is called for.
YOGHURT we use plain full-cream yoghurt unless stated otherwise.
greek plain yoghurt strained in a cloth (traditionally muslin) to remove the whey and to give it a creamy consistency.

CONVERSION CHART

MEASURES

One Australian metric measuring cup holds approximately 250ml; one Australian metric tablespoon holds 20ml; one Australian metric teaspoon holds 5ml. The difference between one country's measuring cups and another's is within a two- or three-teaspoon variance, and will not affect your cooking results. North America, New Zealand and the United Kingdom use a 15ml tablespoon.

All cup and spoon measurements are level.

The most accurate way of measuring dry ingredients is to weigh them.

When measuring liquids, use a clear glass or plastic jug with the metric markings.

We use extra-large eggs with an average weight of 60g.

DRY MEASURES

metric	imperial
15g	½oz
30g	1oz
60g	2oz
90g	3oz
125g	4oz (¼lb)
155g	5oz
185g	6oz
220g	7oz
250g	8oz (½lb)
280g	9oz
315g	10oz
345g	11oz
375g	12oz (¾lb)
410g	13oz
440g	14oz
470g	15oz
500g	16oz (1lb)
750g	24oz (1½lb)
1kg	32oz (2lb)

LIQUID MEASURES

metric	imperial
30ml	1 fluid oz
60ml	2 fluid oz
100ml	3 fluid oz
125ml	4 fluid oz
150ml	5 fluid oz
190ml	6 fluid oz
250ml	8 fluid oz
300ml	10 fluid oz
500ml	16 fluid oz
600ml	20 fluid oz
1000ml (1 litre)	1¾ pints

LENGTH MEASURES

metric	imperial
3mm	⅛in
6mm	¼in
1cm	½in
2cm	¾in
2.5cm	1in
5cm	2in
6cm	2½in
8cm	3in
10cm	4in
13cm	5in
15cm	6in
18cm	7in
20cm	8in
22cm	9in
25cm	10in
28cm	11in
30cm	12in (1ft)

OVEN TEMPERATURES

The oven temperatures in this book are for conventional ovens; if you have a fan-forced oven, decrease the temperature by 10-20 degrees.

	°C (Celsius)	°F (Fahrenheit)
Very slow	120	250
Slow	150	300
Moderately slow	160	325
Moderate	180	350
Moderately hot	200	400
Hot	220	425
Very hot	240	475

The imperial measurements used in these recipes are approximate only. Measurements for cake pans are approximate only. Using same-shaped cake pans of a similar size should not affect the outcome of your baking. We measure the inside top of the cake pan to determine sizes.

INDEX

MINI GINGERBREAD HOUSE TEMPLATES, RECIPE PAGE 218

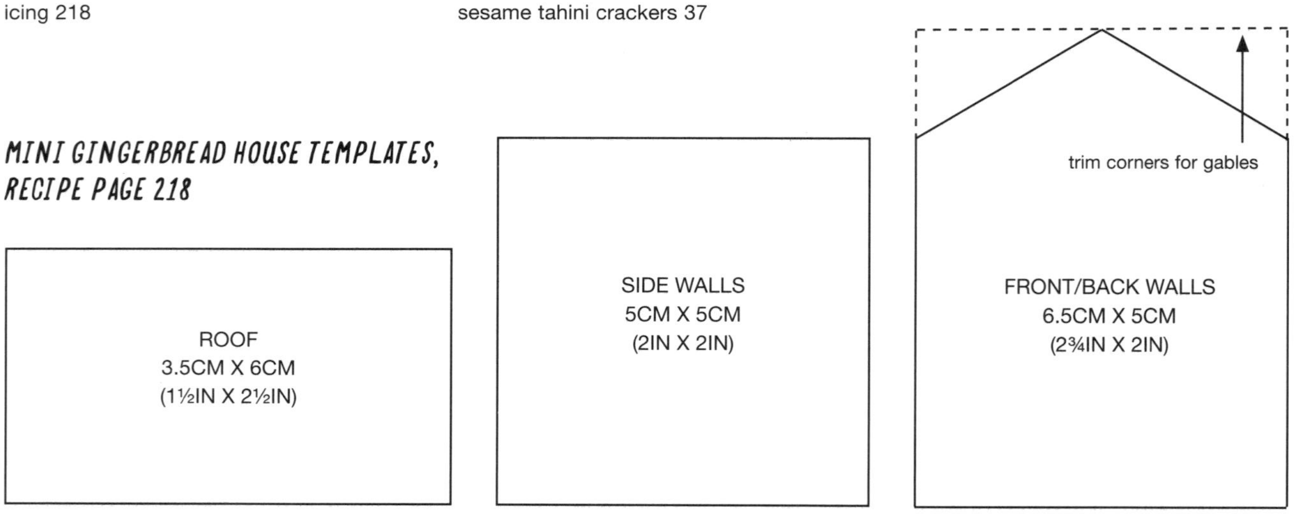